CONTENTS

INTRODUCTION

By Lola T. Small

Western society has made significant strides toward gender parity in recent decades; however, the same progress has yet to be seen for a specific segment of the female population: women of color. Asian women, Latina women, Black women, and Indigenous women often remain at the bottom rung of the ladder when it comes to representation, access, recognition, and power. Is this because we are less intelligent or hardworking or we don't want to be seen, heard, or valued? Or is that the proverbial table only made for those with lighter skin is the one attempting to lead our societies and solve issues that affect our multi-racial communities—even though they have not walked in our shoes.

It is time for a seismic shift in amplifying women of color, a population deep in insight and wisdom from navigating complex and intricate lives. Real change and upward growth can only happen when we take in all perspectives and narratives that make up the world we live in. Experiences of struggle, resilience, triumph, and success that have historically been excluded can become powerful catalysts for inspiration and transformation if we create the space to elevate them. To center women of color as agents and leaders of influence and change can remarkably advance our quests for more justice, equity, synergy, and love.

We Rise in Power aims to increase the representation of voices of women of color as inspiration, influence, empowerment, and leadership. The lived experiences and guidance contained in this anthology will spark women from communities of color to share themselves with more courage, to unapologetically take up more space, and to support each other as we all work toward collective success. Women of color everywhere will know the power of their presence, simply by sharing their initiatives and visionary actions. Readers who are true allies will listen intently to the words here and consciously make space to amplify them.

Our mission is to see more women of color in leadership roles and public media, influencing major social decisions and being respected and celebrated as thought leaders.

Once told to keep our heads down, to not cause too much noise, to smile and look cute in size two, and to bear the blame for whatever society shames, we as Asian women, Latina women, Black women, and Indigenous women are standing up to stake a claim in this new era, to create a more equitable world for ourselves and our children. This is our revolution, and we are opening up to tough conversations around the social issues that matter to all of us and using our voices to light up the next generation. We are here to make an impact and find a way forward.

Women of color advocates, warriors, risk-takers, rule breakers, and gamechangers: we are cranking up the volume for a better future! Let's step onto the stage and make this new world possible.

CHAPTER ONE

BROWN GIRL
IN THE ARENA

*"We live in a world where the color
of our skin announces us before we
even use our voices. How then can we
discover our spark and fire up our voices
for positive change and purpose?"*

Stacey Luces

https://evolutionexecutivecoaching.com
ig: @evolutionexecutivecoaching
fb: @EvolutionExecutiveCoach
li: @staceyluces
t: @staceyluces
Goodreads: @staceyluces

Stacey Luces

Two years ago, on a sunny Friday afternoon Stacey got a call from Lisa, a best-selling author and executive. She told Stacey, "I'm overwhelmed from being sandwiched between work, taking care of my kids and aging parents, I worry about money, my health, and I keep thinking it's too late for me to achieve my goals." Together they evaluated everything on Lisa's plate, created an inspired mindset, and determined gaps. Three months later, Lisa thanked Stacey because she now feels confident, has a plan for growing her career and ensuring her family is cared for, and wakes up every day feeling healthy, happy, and hopeful.

That's what Stacey Luces does. With over twenty-five years of entrepreneurial, executive leadership, strategic planning, and project management expertise, as well as an MBA and a BS in marketing (international business), she works with executives, business owners, and entrepreneurs across the world and helps women feel confident in their ability to live the life of their dreams. Her acumen includes working at the U.S. Department of Homeland Security, the Department of Defense (Pentagon), IBM, Pepsi, Bank of America, and Morgan Stanley.

Sparking impactful change—globally and locally—is important to Stacey. Having grown up in a developing country (Trinidad and Tobago) and traveled extensively across the world, she knows that empowering women changes lives. She has served on the Board of Directors for the United Nations Women (USA, Miami), the Women's Forum at FEMA, and the Women's Foundation of Florida. She lives in Florida with her husband Kevin and their children Alyssa and Adam.

MUD

"The validation of your dreams is not in the color of your skin but in the quality of your heart."

-Kingsley Opuwari Manuel

"Why is your skin so muddy?"

Women of color live in a world where the color of our skin announces our "differentness" before we even use our voices. How then can we discover our spark and fire up our voices for positive change and purpose? The first time I felt my "differentness" was as a teenager. My family and I immigrated to the United States of America in the steamy summer month of June in the early '90s. My sister and I shared a suitcase, and we all slept on borrowed mattresses on the floor of the home of a distant relative. It was also when I was harassed for the first time, and by a ten-year-old, no less. We were in New Jersey at a buffet-style fast food place. I was in line, and he looked at me and said, "Why is your skin so muddy?" I felt uninvited. Unwelcomed. Unwanted. I also felt shocked, exposed, confused, and for the first time in my life, uncomfortable in my own skin—as if something was wrong with me. Then I felt a nudge that I had to change to "fit in." When the world subtly (or not so subtly) signals to us we must change or adapt who we are in order to fit in, to have value, or to belong, or that our dreams are too big, complex, too exotic we shy away from our life's purpose.

Over the years, signals of my "differentness" would be sent in other ways, most significantly in the corporate world. The signals I received there that I was not welcome at the boardroom table, with my "different" viewpoints that would be ignored or worse, casually re-purposed by another, sent the message, "Who do you think you are, with your opinions and intellect and the audacity to challenge the norm?" As women of color, we are no strangers to the rife harassment that makes us feel uncomfortable or disregarded. In my case, these feelings led to a constant pressure for me to fit in, to always perform at my best, to be "seen" as valuable instead of being seen by my skin color only. I came to believe that I had to always work hard for what I wanted in life, that life was a battle, and that I had to conquer it to win. These feelings also made me unstoppable; as the years went by, I strove to define my identity by my intelligence. In any room, I could sit with the best of them and be seen as an expert. I got a series of promotions that led to travel, sixty-hour work weeks, and living to provide rather than living a life of joy and happiness—and I felt incredibly empty and unfulfilled inside. While it has been a beautiful success story financially, spiritually and emotionally, it was an empty reward.

It took me years to understand that this emptiness stemmed from my fear of failure and unworthiness, of being seen through a muddy lens instead of for my heart—my capacity for love, light, and compassion. It also took a toll on my health. After almost losing my life and needing emergency surgery, I hit a wall hard. It was a brutal reality check that left me winded and broken, unsure how to pick up the pieces.

How many of you, like I was, are running a million miles a day trying to prove your worth and value? Are you, in your quiet moments, screaming on the inside, wanting to be heard and asking, "Who am I, what's my purpose, am I worthy, is this all there is to my life?"

Perhaps what we really want to do is run into the ocean, scream with laughter, watch fireworks, feel drunk on life (not wine), know that we already belong—first and foremost—to ourselves. Perhaps the truth of it all is that we are already beautiful and worthy and ready to be unleashed.

Is there a dream or idea that you've not explored or voiced or taken out gently and looked at with hope and wonder? Do you question whether you are courageous or smart enough for big dreams? Do you worry about failing and about what others will say? Are you looking at your own life through a muddy lens? As women of color, living a life worthy of our dreams can seem daunting, but you have the universal right to pursue what makes you happy. Everything you need is already within you. You are unusually incredible, and your courage can ignite others and start a flow of transformation. Isn't it time to find your spark, your voice, and your purpose to create change? Isn't it time to change the lens and live an extraordinary life in a kaleidoscope of color?

Kaleidoscope

"Life on this Earth may be likened to a great Kaleidoscope before which the scenes and facts and material substances are ever shifting and changing, and all anyone can do is to take these facts and substances and rearrange them in new combinations."

-Napoleon Hill

When I was young, I did not have a care in the world. I used to run a lot. Fast. Everywhere. My mom would constantly yell at me to stop, but the wind in my curls, slapping along my calves, making my eyes water, just felt too good. I would slow down till I was out of her eyesight and then speed up again like a little engine that had important things to do. I was happy.

At our core, we all want to belong, be loved, be happy, live on purpose, and make a difference. Somewhere, though, that little girl forgot her values and what she truly loved. She became scared by the opinions of others, the need for conformity; she became overwhelmed with trying to climb the corporate ladder, fit in, be enough. When the way you live is incongruent with your deepest purpose and values, you feel disconnected and empty, and things rarely feel in flow.

What can "pursuing your life's purpose" look like for women of color? Our experiences are often vastly different and indelibly more complex than others'. We often wonder if we even have the time to find our purpose. Even in college, I did not have the time to socialize like other people. I worked two jobs to pay for tuition and was responsible for helping my parents with bills. As I reflected on my values and experiences, it also dawned on me that incredible women (and men) of color helped me get my first job, set up an email account in Hotmail (dating myself here), apply for colleges, and write a resume. They mentored me and recommended life coaches. There was always someone willing to help me, and it showed me that regardless of our past experiences with others, there are amazing humans out there who have expertise, empathy, and a willingness to serve and help you as well. This inspired me to again seek help to close the gap between where I was to where I needed to be.

My own help came in the form of executive coaching, getting clarity on my values, and shifting my mindset so I could more easily separate the things I was doing that did not serve me from the ones that fulfilled my true values. This enabled me to understand how to fill in the gaps to grow. I relocated to another state so I could be closer to the ocean, adjusted my job so I could have better balance, finally listened to my inner voice, and pursued my passion of starting my own business to help empower women to lead more fulfilling, rewarding, and positive lives. I was able to reclaim my time, make deeper connections with those I loved, see my business flourish, lose thirty pounds (which I had been struggling with for over fifteen years), and reverse the symptoms of an autoimmune diagnosis, all within a few months. I also launched my own coaching practice to help other women—and women of color especially—lead more fulfilling lives and pursue things that lit their souls on fire.

Having clearer values also enabled me to join better networks and communities with like-minded people but also with people who differed from me. This is where our true capacity to shine and contribute takes fire; networks that do not look or think like us accelerate our growth and capacity for resilience, whether it's in global foundations or local mentorship. There are inspiring people and communities out there that are designed to create different pathways for us, that encourage us to do more and to give back.

You can change from a life of complacency, overwhelm, and unfulfilment to create a life of happiness and joy, one in which you don't need to change to fit in and get the love you deserve. To do this, we need to identify strategies and ask the right questions to help us get from here to there.

1)   Get clarity

- Look at the imperatives in your life (family, health, wealth, spirituality, etc.). How are you nurturing what is truly important to you?
- How's your mindset? What do you say to yourself when no one's listening?
- Where do you spend your time, and is it making you happy? Are you a human "doing" instead of a human "being"?
- If where you are is not where you want to be, what has to change for you to close the gap? What do you need to stop doing? What needs to happen?

2)   Get confidence

- Is your self-care grounded in love, vitality, and spirituality?
- Are your relationships and networks strong?
- Are your actions (professional and personal) aligned with your values?

3)   Get certainty

- Do you have a strong plan and path for the future?
- Who are the people who have influence over you and over whom you have influence? How can they help?

- Are you prepared for the unexpected?
- How can you remain accountable to the most important person in the world—yourself?

The thing about an aligned value system, a clear sense of purpose, and a focused mindset is that once you decide on your path forward, the universe conspires to give you what you need—if you are open to it. Evaluating where you are now (in your relationships, finances, or health) and envisioning your desired future allows you to plan to close the gap. If the path you're on isn't working, change your direction. If you want something intensely enough, you will find a way to get it. You are worthy and infinitely capable of changing any circumstance in your life for the better.

The Arena

> *"It is not the critic who counts . . . the credit belongs to the man who is actually in the arena, whose face is marred by dust and sweat and blood; who strives valiantly; who errs, who comes short again and again . . . who spends himself in a worthy cause; who at the best knows in the end the triumph of high achievement, and who at the worst, if he fails, at least fails while daring greatly. . ."*
>
> -Theodore Roosevelt

There were many times in my life when I epically failed and felt like I did not matter, like what I did made no difference. I wondered what the point of it was—life, work, trying. It seemed like it would never be enough. I would compare myself to others who seemed to have it all together, wondering what the heck was wrong with me. And sometimes I opted out. Out of the conversation. The situation. The challenge. Let someone else do it. Which ultimately made me feel even worse. In the end, I had to do the emotional and spiritual growth to get myself from where I was to where I needed to be to do the things I wanted to do.

It is easy to sit on the sidelines, to blame, make excuses, procrastinate, and not try. It's safe and a guarantee that you will be successful—*at not accomplishing what you want to accomplish in this one life.* We stay busy, and overwhelmed, and distracted, and ashamed of failing, and so we don't even start. And man, it feels hollow; it yawns like a dark, empty, and painful missed opportunity. This is how we live a life full of regrets. Regret that we let what others think (or may think) stop us from being big, taking up space, amplifying our ideas, trying and failing, and trying and failing and learning all along the way.

We hear a lot about recreating ourselves, pursuing our dreams, igniting our passion. What does it really mean, anyway? I believe that inside every one of you is a burning desire to make a difference. To matter. To have purpose. To do something remarkable with your life. To help others. And if not, this may actually not be the place for you. The women who picked up this particular book *are* here on purpose. They are on fire, every one of them. They want purpose. It may feel muddy and unfocused right now; it may feel like a kaleidoscope—chaotic but beautiful. But you have to be in the arena for it to count. You have to actually SHOW UP. For yourself, your dreams, your purpose, for others. You do not get to judge what others are doing if you are not even trying. We don't care about what those people (or you, if this describes you) think or say or feel.

Growing up in a developing country was a blessing. It taught me the value of gratitude. For water. For electricity. For education. For a community. Navigating the challenges of being an immigrant honed my courage and determination to make it. For my family. My future. My children. And their children. You see, when you hang your dreams on a higher purpose, it becomes an imperative, not an option. What experiences are you grateful for? What strengthened your capacity for taking a leap and believing the net will appear? What almost broke you but honed your ability to navigate change like a champ? What is your higher purpose? Why are you here? If you were to believe that you are already unique and loved by virtue of just being alive and able to make an impact—because innately, everything you actually need is already within you—what would be next? What's your plan?

Many people ask how I have the time to run a business, be on the board for organizations that help the world be a better place, take care of my family, and still be balanced. As women of color, we have to do our part to create spaces for more justice, equity, healing, and connection. By sharing our struggles, our gifts, and our voices, we can stand firm in the arena, knowing that we have the power to make a difference for our communities. I challenge you to rise, rise in love, rise in spirit, rise in gratitude, and use your voices, influence, and networks to take action and make incremental improvements in the world we live in.

Contribution to something larger than yourself will elevate your confidence, clarity, and certainty that you are here on purpose and can make a difference. Even if you start small. Even if it is for one person. Many times we feel like we have to make a big bang to make an impact. But what if you create a small, beautiful ripple that is felt for years? Many people think that they have to be wealthy to contribute, but your wealth could be in your intellect or your ability to bring people together, to analyze data, to write, to listen, to organize. Where and how can you apply those gifts? That is your wealth. That is your power. Unleash that into a mastermind, find and follow folks you admire, get a coach, be a coach, mentor, do *something*. Just start.

Together, we shift the levers from fear, insecurity, and feeling unwelcome to feeling safe, heard, and welcomed. We can do it. You can do it. In fact, I think some of you may already be doing it. It matters. You are making a difference. And you get to change the game. You get to help create a world where no one calls us muddy.

CHAPTER TWO

THE CHOICES WE MAKE

"Choose joy every day and create a life of intention and your own choice. Embrace all that the day offers as tomorrow is not promised to anyone."

Debra Christmas

www.stilettogladiators.com
www.womenintechtribe.com

ig: @womenintechtribe, @xmaswindmill
li: @debrachristmas
t: @WITT2020@, @DRKChristmas

Debra Christmas

Debra Christmas is the co-author of *Please Stay: How Women in Tech Survive and Thrive.* She is the co-founder of Women in Tech Tribe and the founder of Stiletto Gladiators, a non-profit organization focused on diversity and leadership consulting, leadership development and offering coaching and mentorship services for women, with particular emphasis on women in technology. She has worked with hundreds of leaders in her forty-three-year career in technology.

Debra is an executive coach and champion of women and diversity, committed to driving change for women and particularly women of color. She is an educator and a student of leadership, as well as an experienced facilitator of leadership development programs across the globe. Debra is Senior Executive Partner with the global IT research company, Gartner Canada, where she works with leaders across multiple industries on their strategy, their technology decisions, and their own professional development in leading their teams through digital disruption and relentless change. She is also writing two additional books on leadership and encouraging girls to choose technology as a career.

Debra lives in Hamilton, Ontario with her husband Wayne. Their blended family consists of six children, eight grandchildren, and two chihuahuas, Milo and Luna.

As a Black woman born in 1957 in Montreal, Canada, I was taught at a very young age about choices. Like many Black children, male and female, I was taught to carry myself a certain way, to speak the Queen's English, to be careful about who I associated with, to pay attention to my surroundings, to be powerful with my words, to let no one identify me over the telephone as a Black person, to work hard, to work harder than everyone else as I needed to be twice as good to be considered equal, to dress with elegance, to straighten my hair, and to minimize my ethnicity when outside our family home, when away from our community. These were choices my parents dictated, and I embraced them in my younger years. I did exactly what I was told; that was the norm for the decade I was born into. The choices served me well. I was able to navigate the public school system, university, and my corporate career by putting into action those choices and many more.

Sixty-five years later, I still think about choice every single day. Consciously I choose joy every day regardless of what is put in my path. I wake up happy and I celebrate the many blessings bestowed upon me. This doesn't mean being a "Pollyanna;" it simply means I put things in perspective. I ask myself if something will matter in five years, or five months, or even five days. I am intentional in my thoughts, my words, and most importantly my actions. Careful thought goes towards the impact of what I do, and even though it can be exhausting on so many levels, I cannot imagine living any other way. This doesn't mean I cannot be spontaneous. It doesn't mean I cannot be creative, or silly, or intense. What it does mean is that I recognize as a Black woman that every single choice I make has a ripple effect. And the more conscious I am of what those ripples look like, the better equipped I am to address whatever comes my way. This strategy has worked incredibly well for me and the life I have chosen to live. Let me share why it might be a path for you as well.

Life is about choices. We make dozens of choices a day, hundreds a week, thousands a month. Could we even count the choices and decisions we make in our lifetime? It would be like guessing how many jellybeans there are in a jar. Our lives are anchored in choices and decisions, and not all of them are created equal. When we make choices and decisions, from the smallest, most innocuous things, like what I am going to wear today or what am I going to make for dinner, to the biggest and most impactful, such as who I will choose as a life partner or whether I will have children, there is a downstream impact. Those choices have their individual trajectory, and running underneath them are emotions, family dynamics, societal influences, life experiences, stories in our head, and much more. Some choices we give little thought to, while others we languish over. Regardless of the process, the timeline, the underpinnings that influence us, it behooves every single one of us Black women to think strategically about the choices we make. Why? Because we are held to a different standard. We are scrutinized at a level that might be hard to describe. Society has an impression of Black women, and it is more negative than it is positive. The oppressor mired it in history, slavery, misogyny, misconceptions, imagery, fantasy, fetishes, pop culture, and much more. We are always judged.

Our society lives in judgment. We live in a society that scrutinizes and judges on so many levels. All of us, male and female, have something to say about everything and everyone. Many things that we comment on are not our business. We feel we are entitled to share our perspective. We think we have a right to tell someone that they are not doing something right, that their choices should be different. We all do this. Regardless of whether we think we are, we are judging; we are comparing something or someone with a filter that was created and cultivated from the time we were very young based on the home we were raised in, the culture we are part of, or the norms and customs of our socialization. We criticize, complain and judge. It is the human experience for all of us, but those judgments play out differently for Black people, particularly Black women. We live in a society that looks at us differently. The world has been taught that the color of our skin comes with judgment. If you look different from the majority, there is judgment. If you speak differently from the majority, there is judgment. If you behave differently from the majority, there is judgment. There are barriers and systems that work against you. Those judgments are built into processes and systems that we need to navigate. Why? Because as Black women, we live in a constant state of being judged. The way we walk, the way we carry ourselves, the way we dance, our gestures, our words, our clothes, and God knows, our hair. Every aspect of our wonderful selves is subject to scrutiny.

The reality is that the Black woman is strong, resilient, competent, funny, beautiful, brash, and so many more wonderful descriptors. I was so very fortunate to have incredible role models in my life. Fabulous, bold, kind, competent, highly capable, smart Black women—my mother, my grandmother, my godmother, my aunts—all of whom made such an impact in my world.

I was born to a white mother and a Black father, both nineteen years old. I was born out of wedlock. What an awful term. My birth mother came from the small town of Granby, Quebec. I recently found her, but I never knew her. I was raised by my father's family and never knew my birth mother's side. My father was born and raised in Montreal. He was handsome, vivacious, known as "The Prince." With his magnificent ebony skin and smile that could light up a room, his presence would fill a space. But he was not equipped to raise a child, so his mother, my grandmother, decided I should be raised by his family. She instructed my father to "go get the child and bring her to us." A choice that changed the course of my life.

It didn't happen immediately. A family friend took me in as a young infant. She and her husband were planning to adopt me when my father's sister decided she needed to raise her brother's child and retrieved me and raised me as their own. How she convinced her husband of less than a year to take me in, I will never know, especially since he and my father did not get along (despised each other actually). That choice set in motion a domino effect that I still feel to this day. Even though the tension between my two fathers created many challenges in my life, I am grateful for my mother's love and generosity. She raised me with sound principles, values, and opportunities. The extended family created an experience I treasure. But their choices came at a price. The choices of the adults who controlled my world have affected me to this very day. We rarely consider the generational consequences of our choices, particularly when they are not well thought out. Sometimes when good people choose what they think is a good thing, it doesn't always play out well.

My family chose to operate in secrecy, without clear communication and honesty regarding my birth circumstances and certainly without knowing what could materialize thirty, forty, or fifty years later. We often underestimate and misunderstand the power of choice. An important factor in becoming ourselves is learning and understanding that choices—our own and of others'—have impacts, both positive and negative. For me, it came through exploration, deep reflection, and therapy to understand that choices do not have to define us for the rest of our lives. We can change the trajectory of our life if we understand this powerful thing called choice.

As a young, caramel-skinned girl with bright eyes, a big smile, and a pleasant disposition, I assimilated easily into the world. I learned I was adopted and that changed everything. Sensing that something was different, I looked nothing like my sisters, and people commented about that. When we found out together that I was adopted, my younger sister realized she was, in fact, the oldest and told me I should go back to where I came from. She was just seven years old, but I never forgot those words. They cut me to the core. I was only ten, and I truly feared my parents would return me to my birth mother. I thought that if I didn't behave, they might send me back, so I made choices at a very young age that I thought could save me from that fate. I would be perfect. I would be whatever my family wanted me to be. I would make them so proud. I knew how to be flexible; I had the ability to adapt quickly to my surroundings. I fit in. I was pleasant, happy, cheerful, and driven. I was polite and well-spoken. I was well-behaved and capable of doing anything I set my mind to. I followed the rules, both my family's rules and those of the community I had come to love.

In both communities, Black and white, I fit in, and to the outside world, I didn't appear Black—or at least I heard the ridiculous comment, "I don't ever think of you as Black." At school, I was told my features were too fine to be a Black person; I must be Eurasian. What does that even mean? That I wasn't threatening? That I didn't fit a stereotype? That I wasn't like other Black people they knew? I never asked. I didn't give it a second thought. I simply showed up every day, focused on school or my job, and got things done.

I didn't pretend to be something I wasn't and never struggled with my identity. When I looked in the mirror, I saw a Black girl/woman looking back at me, and I belonged to a strong Black family and community who taught me to be extremely achievement-driven and committed to excellence. I was raised without the traditional gender constraints of "girls do this and boys do that," which in itself was rare in that time. I was raised to know right from wrong and was taught to stand up for myself, to anyone at any time. Even as a young girl, I had the courage to stand up for myself and take on anyone who called me names or tried to bully me (and many did).

That courage muscle was well developed by the time I headed off to university at seventeen years old. My voice was strong, and I used it—often. I was not afraid to speak up, even if there was risk involved. I focused on my studies and would let nothing interfere with my academic performance. My parents expected me to deliver good grades and to not disappoint them. I was the first in my family to go to university and the only one to obtain a university degree. It wasn't just about me; I was representing my family and my community. Very few young people in my world moved away from home to pursue an education, and they were all watching me. I did not disappoint. I think my parents' and my grandparent's happiest moment was seeing me walk across the stage to receive my degree.

I am told over the years I have mellowed a bit, and I am not as intimidating as I used to be—never had I thought of myself as either of those adjectives. I was simply doing what I thought was right for me, with aspiration, intention, and a plan. Being a focused person, I operate with intention. And I have always had a plan—my own professional development plan. When I started a new job, I would think about where it could take me, what the next opportunity could be. I always made sure I understood the organization, figuring out who was who, where the seat of power was held, who had influence, where I could shine and deliver value. I was ambitious, intentional, and involved in my work. Special initiatives like diversity, equity, and inclusion raised my visibility. At any level of the organization, I offered my perspective openly. I never looked at authority figures as smarter or more important than I was; they just did a different job. If anything, I paid attention to how they did what they did so I could learn from them. I was forthright and asked very specific questions about jobs, opportunities, and career options. Asking questions gave me further insights into how the organization worked. I paid attention to nuances, who was connected to whom, where there appeared to be alliances. I was incredibly curious and would also share my thoughts and was truthful in my communications and that was well received and respected. Position or title did not intimidate me. I had confidence instilled in me from a young girl that has served me well my entire career.

What was key is my confidence did not play out as arrogant, angry, or overly assertive, so they could receive it relatively well. That is not always the case for Black women. The rules are different for us. When we are direct, they consider us too outspoken. When we are forthright and speak honestly, we are perceived as aggressive. When we call out bad behavior, we are seen as angry. This might apply to women in general, but there is a heightened sensitivity when Black women are the main character.

So what do we do? How do we move forward? By being intentional with our choices. By having a plan. As hard as it can be to be intentional, to give careful thought to what you do, how you walk in the world, and who you connect with, it can also be a lightning rod of accelerated effort and a beacon of light that guides your path. While all kinds of things can happen serendipitously in our lives, amazing things happen when you think about what outcomes you hope to achieve and what needs to happen to secure success—however you define it. We live in a system of interconnected parts and if we don't think about that ripple in the pond, if we don't think about where a choice can take us, how can we course correct or carve out a new path that can get us where we aspire to go?

Choices also mean accountability. We are accountable for everything we say and do, and being conscious about that accountability is a choice. Choice about how you want to live, about who you choose to share your life with, about the principles and values you choose to live by. These are essential choices in the life journey you have embarked upon.

One enlightening way to look at this journey is to create a life journey map laying out the choices you've made. Start from high school. What did you choose to do as you were completing school? What choices did you make from that point on? What possibilities were in front of you and what did you decide to do? Which of those choices have served you well? Which created a domino effect you were not prepared for? If you could talk to your younger self, knowing what you know now, would you tell her to make the same choices?

If you are young and just getting started, being more deliberate in charting your course can deliver benefits beyond your wildest dreams. Bringing into focus those big dreams, those aspirational goals, and thinking about what it might take to get there is an exercise well worth doing—especially for a Black woman. Your life stage can be as big, as bold, as magnificent as you want it to be. You just need to be focused on those choices.

Don't let anyone derail you. There will be naysayers, but there will also be champions. There will be guides, coaches, rescuers, and supporters. Recognize the difference, watch for them all, and forge ahead focused and committed to your dreams. Pay attention to the choices of others, understand how they impact you, and learn from every interaction. Every choice makes a difference, and there is a difference in the choices we make.

Choose well.

CHAPTER THREE

TO RISE ABOVE THE CONVENTIONAL

"I am unconstrained by anyone else's version of success because I am an original and so is my journey."

Sherry S. Maharaj

ig: @shermaharaj
fb: @shermaharaj
li: @shermaharaj

Sherry S. Maharaj

Sherry S. Maharaj is passionate about creating positive social change. She serves as an executive on the Board of Directors of the BBNC which helps diverse individuals, families, and communities to overcome barriers and enhance their quality of life. She leverages corporate engagement to provide training and internship programs for youth in marginalized communities, founded the ForwardStart initiative to work collaboratively with government and volunteer agencies in supporting employment and integration for newcomers in regulated professions, and she leads the OnBoarded committee to promote equity, diversity, and inclusion in the boardroom, through mentoring and leadership opportunities for women. As a lawyer and managing partner, she provides solutions for businesses to navigate international trade, immigration, intellectual property and project management by implementing socially responsible standards across jurisdictions.

Sherry also enjoys biographies, paddling on a competitive dragonboat team, and spending time with her family.

S omebody once tried to teach me that if I always do what is easy, my life would be hard but if I do what is hard, my life could be easy. The path of least resistance was very convenient, but eventually I learned how to do hard things. It was easy: I just needed to get comfortable being un-comfortable and wake up every day with the courage to not be stunted by failure.

While still navigating my formative years, I abruptly removed myself from everything that was dear to me and fled to a new country, alone. When I arrived from life in the tropics into the midst of winter, the only sensation I felt was relief. It was as though I had untangled myself from the chokehold of my secret shame. Nobody here knew that I regarded my life as a colossal disaster since I'd spectacularly failed to achieve my one and only ambition.

It had been inculcated into me from a young age that I should get an education. I might have embraced law as my only option because everyone I knew bought into the notion that law was an upper class privilege and I might as well study it since I had the brains. But from the onset of my mid-teenage years, I became dis-tracted. My previously stellar academic performance rapidly de-generated into mediocrity, culminating in my failure to gain early admission to study law. I considered rectifying the conundrum of my academic nosedive by repeating my examinations to get back on track. It wasn't that I had lofty ideals of becoming a lawyer to make a ton of money or save the world; it was that girls from my neighborhood did not grow up to become lawyers—in fact, most did not finish high school—and I had been given an opportunity to attend a prestigious school and defy that stereotype. I wanted to champion that cause and prove our competence. However, the thought of enduring another year at that school to improve my grades made me too uncomfortable and I opted to take the easier way out. I hastily settled for a place in the program of my second choice.

Off to university I went. I started off strong and was on the precise trajectory to accomplish all that was expected of me. Then I faltered. Again. I preferred to party all night and sleep all day. I neglected to attend classes or apply myself but still passed all my courses with high grades, until the second-to-last semester when I flippantly dropped out of school. There was no valid reason. There was no plan to do anything else. I simply did not attempt to stick it out. I quit. Somebody must have tried to advise me to hang in there, as I was over three-quarters of the way finished, but it is highly likely that I did not care to hear it. It was too easy to avoid challenging myself. I wrote a long letter about my decision that was never delivered to anyone. I did not need to save myself from famine or war or human rights abuses; what I needed was to escape the feeling that my life was going nowhere because I was not doing what I had originally hoped. Short-sightedness got the better of me and in a counter-intuitive move, I bailed on my formal education.

After a cooling-off period, I thought about returning to school but I had more pertinent issues to occupy my mind, such as finding employment in order to afford life in the developed world. Technology jobs were plentiful when I entered the workforce, and the pay was more than I had ever had, but I was limited to menial tasks because I lacked a piece of paper to confirm that I graduated from anything beyond high school in a third world region. I wanted to do more but enrolling in any type of schooling was a terrifying idea. After all, I had already attempted a degree and failed to follow through; I wondered if I was even capable of finishing one. Then there was the cost. I had no right to ask for financial assistance after the stunt I had pulled. My people had worked multiple jobs to pay for an education that I abandoned. Now I would have to bear all expenses by myself, which meant that I needed additional jobs on top of the two I was already working. Instead, I chose to forego higher paying positions until I gained enough experience, but it was difficult to gain that experience when I did not have the requisite education to secure jobs that would provide the experience.

Due to the financial constraints and mounting pressure (from myself) to make progress, I resolved to teach myself. Information was everywhere; I borrowed books from the public library, scoured the internet for tutorials, and even made a schedule to school myself. That started off rough because there was no institution threatening to reprimand me for not following my timetable: it was solely up to me to do or not do. Whenever I rose above my excuses, though, I was able to advance. Bit by bit, I acquired knowledge and skills that translated into multiple certifications. I was not always consistent but I grew accustomed to putting in short bursts of intensive study and successfully completing the corresponding tests. I went so far as to take the LSAT, and the impressive result made me believe that I might be destined for the study of law after all. I knew that people before me had fulfilled their ambition of going to school while working, so it was possible—somehow.

With minimal preparation, I banked on my high LSAT score and applied for admission to the one law school I had set my sights on. A prompt reply wished me good luck in my future endeavors. I was gutted. That rejection became justification for not submitting any other applications. I convinced myself that I did not feel like completing an undergraduate degree, after which I would have to dedicate at least three whole years to law school, followed by almost another year of articling. I wanted to be a lawyer, but it would just take too much of my effort and time.

Time progressed, and so did my know-how and job responsibilities. With an entrepreneurial spirit, I quickly worked my way up the employment ranks. All my jobs came from referrals and in almost record time, I was managing people who had been working in my industry for as many years as I had been alive. I was fortunate to work with the best and the brightest and I relished those opportunities to learn how they did what they did. Every Monday, I sat in a boardroom with eight wealthy white men who possessed exceptionally impressive credentials and were leaders in their respective fields. I was awestruck to even be in their presence. I listened attentively to the banter about their affluent weekend activities and I looked on in reverence as they made decisive management moves. I always received compliments on my appearance and was often asked to convey kudos to my team, and my salary was more than I would have been earning as a junior lawyer. It was a very easy gig. I thought about law school from time to time but whenever I mentioned law, the sages advised me that I already had a lucrative career. I was told that shelling out funds to go to school now would be a waste of resources; I could invest that money into something else. School would only disrupt my sleep and take energy away from more pleasant pastimes. I was reminded that many people were successful without going to school and amassing crippling student debt. It was easier to stay where I was—and I did.

My innate interest in law steered me toward managing projects for clients in the legal industry. Only the most dire issues were escalated to me and in addressing them, I was required to comprehend lawyer jargon and legal concepts. To make sure I was the best at what I was doing, I started taking evening classes in corporate law. My day job finished at five o'clock in the evening, and class would start at six or seven o'clock. I was fascinated by the intersection of law with everything. My weekday was incomplete until I delved into an interesting legal topic. I was developing a learning habit and a study routine without even noticing it; maybe it was because I thoroughly enjoyed what I was learning and could immediately apply it to benefit my work or maybe because I was not mandated to do it beyond my own pace. The lawyers and law firms who interacted with me appreciated the extra attention, and work life became easier for all of us. One such lawyer who headed up the legal department for a well-known multinational corporation expressed his gratitude to my employer and casually mentioned his opinion that I would make an excellent lawyer. That compliment offended me more than a direct insult. He did not know me; if I was really that intelligent, then I would have gone to law school already. When I attempted to set the record straight, he mocked me by saying that I didn't need to be the smartest to get through law school; I only had to be willing to do the work.

Instead I worked on other life goals. I started a consulting business, hiring legal professionals to execute tasks I was not licensed to perform, and I moved on to providing services to a larger firm. The new scene was exhilarating. Offices were obscenely spacious, lawyers were dressed to impress, and the place buzzed with hushed activity. The services and international client list were very exclusive and my work seemed extremely important: until it didn't. During my last month at that firm, I approached a managing partner with a suggestion for how I could participate in doing business differently. He applauded my foresight but informed me that my kind of thinking would only be relevant if I was one of the decision-makers. As I mulled over that information, it revealed a massive problem. I strategized on how to reach the executive level from my current post. I calculated the number of years I would have to be a cog in the wheel and the sheer volume of talented practitioners who would have to retire in order for me to move on up. It was a daunting prospect. I could have dedicated my entire working life to that firm and still not impacted the company in any significant way. I had a really good job in a really great firm but at my core, I felt that my status quo was not sustainable.

When I looked for guidance, I was strongly influenced by what I did not see. I had not yet come across any colored, immigrant woman who was doing what I proposed to do. I imagined that my life was a movie and wondered what the hero(ine) of that story would do. No doubt she would transform into whatever she desired to be; setbacks would never prevent her from living her dream life. I plotted out how to reach the pinnacle of my career which, for me, would be to lead and facilitate inclusion. I like to listen. I have always been a more interested than interesting teammate. I genuinely believe that each person has something valuable to contribute and I thrive on encouraging others to share their unique gifts and put forward their own best effort. Consequently, I always benefited from supporting other people's success, and that's how I wanted to run my business. The solution was obvious. If I wanted to advocate for access to justice for all and cater to issues affecting my community in languages representing the diversity of my heritage; if I wanted to lead an inclusive law firm where everyone felt valued and uplifted: I needed to create my own.

That meant that I had to go to law school. I also wanted to continue working. Despite my apprehension, I made up my mind to do both—even though there was a possibility that I could fail at one or the other, or both. I mustered up the courage to put myself out there again. I took the time to carefully tailor my applications. I was a much more competitive candidate this time around but I still hedged my bets by applying to more than one school and to more than one category. My preparation was rewarded with an acceptance letter, but when I read it, I felt sick to my stomach. The offer of admission was conditional on the completion of an undergraduate degree. The bane of my existence, which had never truly ceased to haunt me, came to the fore yet again. I reluctantly reached out to the university I had attended to request to complete the remaining courses required for my degree. They regretfully informed me that too much time had passed since I withdrew without their permission so I would need to reapply for and win admission to that program in order to continue. I contacted other universities to find out if I could apply the courses I had actually completed in order to receive transfer credits toward a degree program. Unfortunately, my foreign university courses were not accredited so I would be required to complete an entire undergraduate program from the beginning.

I started with single courses. Preliminary ones were meant to be the easiest but were actually the ones I struggled with the most. The long commute to and from work left me drained and on some days, especially when darkness came early, it was preferable to head home rather than travel to school. There was no point in feigning understanding when I knew that I hadn't read in preparation for class and was absolutely not following the discussion. I expected summer school to be less arduous, but the long evenings and social scene competed with class attendance. My eyes would sting from tears of frustration as I tried to read and comprehend on my own before attempting assignments and tests. The course content was manageable, but it took more than a few tries over the semesters until I was able to balance my academic and professional workload without doping up on caffeine to stay awake during ungodly hours and avoid passing out from sheer exhaustion.

I had to learn how to manage my time; I also had to teach myself why and then make peace with the short-term sacrifice that was required. With a better attitude and consistent effort, I finally consolidated credits from self-study challenge examinations with some credits from my experiential learning and a few compulsory courses to attain that elusive undergraduate degree, with honors. I realized that no setback can dictate my future, unless I let it. Ultimately, long after the time it would have taken me to finish if I had been brave enough to take the plunge earlier, I found myself in a lecture hall, soaking up the wisdom imparted to me on my first day of law school. I felt like I could do everything I set my heart to and that anything in this world was possible because I was no longer afraid of discomfort. I was free to dream and I was invincible. I knew then that the next chapters of my life would be on my terms.

The ability to truly listen and learn lessons from others is an essential life skill. However, it's extremely easy to get bogged down in noise, so the ability to also listen to your own inner guidance to stay or change course becomes vital. Contrary to all advice, I embarked on a legal education while caring for a family and building a business, and I managed to do it. That was no mean feat; in truth, it was often too overwhelming to handle by myself. I felt guilty that I was not devoting enough time to my family responsibilities. I became frustrated when I didn't achieve my milestones as quickly as I wanted. My attendance at social engagements was almost nil because I had to repurpose that time toward working on my academic and professional goals. I worried that I was being cavalier by leaving the security of my employment to pursue an unrealistic ambition. Sometimes I cried simply because I could not see a light at the end of the tunnel. It was during those times that I had to remind myself there was more than one path to my objective and that I couldn't always see mine because I was creating it with every step that I was taking. All I had to do was keep going. I took stock of my failures and also my successes, and the simple reminder that everything will be okay no matter the outcome inspired my confidence to tackle the next task.

Managing a busy legal services practice while attending law school was a blast. I was even awarded an additional degree after that. It became easy enough to embrace short-term imbalance in order to achieve greater balance overall. I discovered that the more I gave to my goals, the more support I found and each hurdle was progressively easier to surmount. It was a beautiful evolution from a disenchanted adolescent, easily derailed by the minor setback of one bad test score, into that woman who could forge her own path.

There was no fairy godmother magic, and I did not have more hours in my day than anybody else, but I was able to establish and lead my own law firm to provide services across multiple jurisdictions. It did not matter that my journey to becoming a lawyer was unconventional. It did not matter that I didn't come from a privileged background or have pertinent connections. It certainly did not matter that I didn't get it right on the first try. What mattered was that I developed faith in myself, discipline, and the willingness to be resilient.

CHAPTER FOUR

BLAZE YOUR OWN TRAIL

*"By blazing unique trails and crafting
a journey just for us, it puts us in
a position to provide something
truly extraordinary—one-of-a-kind
contributions that no one else can!"*

Nancy Chang

www.mamalaoshi.club
ig: https://www.instagram.com/mamalaoshi
fb: https://www.facebook.com/MamaLaoshi
li: https://www.linkedin.com/in/nancychang8
YouTube: https://www.youtube.com/@MamaLaoshi

Nancy Chang

Nancy Chang is an inquisitive explorer, embracing new possibilities with curiosity. She grew up in Taiwan and is now raising her two daughters in America, she sees herself not as a first-generation immigrant but instead a global citizen building a home with her family at the heart of it. Blending a spirit of adventure with an eye for opportunity, she persistently strives to discover new and creative approaches to the age-old problems that life throws our way.

During her early years, she had the amazing opportunity of working and gaining exposure in different countries as a management consultant at McKinsey. She later earned an MBA from Harvard Business School that inspired her to take on new challenges with more perspective. After working for several years at TripAdvisor, motherhood sparked something within her—An urge to contribute more to this world. She is the co-founder of A Little Chinese, passing down Chinese culture to children and also the producer and host of Mama Laoshi—an educational children's show on a mission to nurture the explorer spirit in young children, guiding them to learn more about both themselves and our wonderful world.

Nancy's journey is far from complete, but with each exploration, the rewards of learning and self-discovery become more profound. She is optimistic and excited for whatever life has in store.

TRAILBLAZER?

I n 2015, when I was a fresh-eyed Harvard Business School grad at my first corporate America tech job, at a year-end company event I received a tiny owl statue from my then-employer that reads,"Nancy Chang - Trail Blazer." Honestly, I can't remember the specific details as to why they awarded me this accolade (I think it was around developing a new ad product that was not commonly done at that time and went against all conventional wisdom), but I've kept that little owl statue on my desk to this day. Despite going from a hip tech company stand-up desk to a messy work-from-home office with video scripts, puppets, and even a breast pump laying around, the word "trailblazing" serves as a motto in my life.

I've always been drawn to creating my own trail instead of following someone else's. I do my best work when I find a path that works better for me—one that brings more joy and allows me to be more authentic. In my twenties, instead of following the well-traveled road to law school graduation and a career in traditional law, I was driven by curiosity to explore different aspects of the world through a job as a business consultant at McKinsey. As a business consultant, I've been lucky enough to work with many interesting people and learn about different sectors. However, my desire to have more impact beyond the for-profit world led me toward exploring the social sector. This eventually led me to an opportunity to work with the leading Asian dance company, Cloud Gate, in Taiwan. At twenty-three years old, I was advising the company founder about how to develop their new dance museum theater—an unique experience different from the conventional business consultant track. I never realized it at the time, but by making those early choices, I was practicing and developing my ability to pave my own path and be more unconventional. These skills were essential when I relocated to

America, a land where I was labeled as a double minority—both female and Asian—and had to navigate unfamiliar cultural norms and environments: starting anew, being imaginative, and finding a direction in which I could uniquely contribute while having limited resources and connections in an unfamiliar country.

Today, if you were to ask me to give a quick intro of myself, I would happily say that I am a playful (and sleep-deprived) burb mother of two beautiful girls, one five years old and the other only five months. Many children and families know me as "Mama Laoshi," which means "mom teacher" in Chinese, due to my educational children's show. Additionally, I am the founder of Mama Laoshi Education Media, a social enterprise dedicated to creating high-quality media content for children and to inspire the explorer spirit alive in every child. My current life is the epitome of #momlife: I'm often spotted wearing a messy bun and work-from-home sweats, trying to sneak in work calls and recording videos during my daughter's nap time. If my younger self, working at the prestigious management consulting firm McKinsey, had seen me now, wearing a green suit and intensely Googling how to make a puppet's mouth move more smoothly for a children's educational video, she would be incredulous. But I believe that this is the beauty of life: it's an ongoing journey full of surprises. By learning to embrace our uniqueness, love our quirks, and find a path that works for us despite the challenges in the world around us, we increase our chances of discovering something that is truly meant for us and allows us to shine.

At this specific moment in life, I am keenly aware that I am still on the journey of finding my place in the world (I'm a "WIP," as they would say from my elite consulting days), but I feel optimistic, energized, and at peace with the strange path I have been on so far. Although I cannot say I have all the answers, compared to my more anxious self ten years ago, I have learned many things about life, paving paths, and how we can feel more at ease knowing that everything will work out as long as we are willing to put ourselves out there. My goal for the rest of the chapter is to share my experiences and what I've learned so far, in the hopes that it will be helpful as you discover your own unique path and voice.

Explore to Gain Perspective

I grew up in Taiwan in a relatively sheltered, homogenous environment, but I was curious about the world beyond my home. Fortunately, my parents were open-minded and encouraged me to explore. It was during my college exchange programs to Hong Kong and the Netherlands that I met people who were dissimilar from me and places that seemed novel at that time. I was able to connect with people from various backgrounds and cultures, which broadened my outlook on life. I'm grateful that we were young then and open-minded to learning about different lifestyles and values. Those early experiences made me realize how similar we all are despite our differences. They also sparked curiosity within me about what makes me unique and how I can make a difference in the world. Moving to the US was a major adjustment for me, as I had to learn and adapt my mindset in order to thrive among its unique culture. It required me stepping outside of my comfort zone if I wanted to truly experience this new setting fully; an improvisational journey that brought much delight when gaining insight into all of the interesting differences between societal systems and cultural norms. Striking out into the unknown gave me an unprecedented opportunity to grow my horizons and inner depths of understanding, not just about our world but myself. Taking stock of both strengths and weaknesses is essential for fully appreciating who we are—without perspective there is no way to forge a meaningful path unique to ourselves.

Reinvent New Paths When You Feel Stuck

Every one of us has a burning curiosity as to what life holds for us, but too often our ambitions are limited by traditional paths others have defined, even more, minorities often find themselves facing numerous barriers and limitations when pursuing more traditional paths—making the journey filled with challenges. Society and our own expectations can often mislead us into thinking that stability and success require one route. However, it's important to remember the importance of honoring ourselves with whatever pathway brings out our true potential. I found this to be true when my family was elated that I had been accepted into a prestigious law school in Taiwan as it seemed like an assured pathway to future security. Yet midway through law school reality set in—it wasn't right for me! Seizing onto what felt more natural, I explored different career avenues which ultimately led me back into the business world where many of my strengths could flourish. This valuable lesson in my early life has stayed with me: follow your gut when you feel a path is not right. It's not to say quit every time there are hurdles, but rather tune into our instincts and be open-minded towards alternate solutions. After all, sometimes the best way forward involves carving out new routes. By taking the initiative to forge our own paths, we can find creative solutions that open up unique possibilities.

Use Your Uniqueness as a Strength

Working at TripAdvisor was my introduction into the American workplace and first time feeling like a minority as I was one of few Asians on an almost entirely US-centric team. As a product manager, it was essential for me to build bridges between various stakeholders; yet at times this meant navigating through unfamiliar language and cultures. When I first started, it was hard not to feel the pressure of having to conform. But with a few inspiring colleagues and mentors in my corner, I began to relax into my identity—which turned out to be an invaluable asset. Thanks to this change-of-heart and being the only international member on our team, I had plenty of opportunities for meaningful contributions that would've otherwise been missed. This experience taught me something important: don't let the fear of being different hold you back when your distinctiveness could open up so many new pathways and opportunities. By pushing ourselves to explore the depths of who we are, uncovering our unique quirks and capabilities, we can open up a new realm of personal growth and awareness. Through understanding these qualities within us that make each one special in their own way, it helps pave an individualized path for future success.

Be Patient While You Piece Together the Puzzle

Becoming a mother was an incredibly impactful moment in my life, and I realized the need to find greater balance between career ambitions and family. After much deliberation on how this could be achieved, I decided to pursue entrepreneurship with higher hopes of being able to create something meaningful while still having quality time with my children. Stepping off the beaten path can be a healthy way to unearth new solutions and grow. Taking the plunge into entrepreneurship gave me a chance to find unique solutions for difficulties I was encountering in my career and it enabled me to take the initiative of creating something that highlighted my skill set, harnessed my aspirations, while still accommodating life as a mom of young children.

When I began, the unknown was quite daunting; but luckily with my partner's support and a network of friends and mentors providing guidance, combined with my cultivated optimism in times of uncertainty—it set me off on an exciting journey into unexplored territory. I allowed myself the freedom to discover hidden aspects of who I am and find uncharted paths that resonated more authentically with my values and desires. As each new possibility presented itself, it felt like one step closer towards reaching those goals most meaningful to me. After a lot of soul-searching, I felt inspired to explore new opportunities within the education sector in order to make this world a more equitable place—something that my heart was guiding me towards. I was also interested in finding ways to integrate my mom-life desires of being present for my children and balancing my career ambitions of contributing to something larger than myself. Stepping into uncharted waters, I found myself without a map or any sure direction, both entrepreneurship and motherhood were new and unchartered territories for me. Patience and openness to learning were the guiding forces on my journey. Even in failure I found valuable wisdom, which helped me listen more closely to my inner voice of guidance. However, the winding road of life is rarely straight, and it can be especially unpredictable during times of adversity, like the pandemic. I found myself having to not only build a business but also homeschool a child—no small feat! Pushing myself to continue on the journey was far from easy, but it enabled me to be more patient and grounded. I drew on my friends and mentors for support, trusting in both their advice and my own instinct. Despite the constraints around us at that time and my occasional despair of not knowing what I was doing, pushing ahead allowed me to explore new possibilities; As I began homeschooling my daughter, a surprise passion blossomed within me: teaching the young generation. It was something that had seemingly come out of nowhere - yet it soon unfolded as one of my greatest interests! As if guided by unseen forces, the idea to inspire children to explore, and to seek opportunities where East could meet West —the idea of Mama Laoshi was born: A motherly teacher inspiring kids all over the world with her Asian heritage! I found a mission and a new path for myself: to nurture the innate sense of exploration that lives within each child and support every parent or caretaker who raises them. The educational content I started producing under Mama Laoshi was informed by developmental science, had cultural influences from both East and West, and importantly crafted with love and care. As I took on the role of host and producer of the children's program, a fresh sense of purpose revealed itself to me. A clearer vision for what lay ahead began to unfold before my eyes. Gaining clarity took not only resilience, but time and patience.

Be Biased Towards Action

After many twists and turns, I find myself doing something that was unimaginable to me three years ago: running my own children's show. Despite the unexpectedness of it all, looking back one lesson stands out—take action! It's not as simple as impulsively jumping in without thought or strategy—it means making thoughtful decisions and being resourceful so that we can shape our future paths with intention. With no steps taken forward, nothing gets achieved!

I'm deeply thankful for the exploration I've done and all of the doors it has opened. Through my pursuit, I've joined filmmaking classes to unleash creativity, reconnected with friends and mentors from prior days, launched a passion business alongside remarkable mothers and lead nonprofit projects supporting child development; each experience providing me profound understanding on what resonates most within myself so that I can carry onward to create my own path forward.

Lean on Others for Support and Inspiration

Navigating the unknown often leaves us feeling overwhelmed and uncertain. But it's important to remember that we're never alone in this journey; having a trusted mentor or companion is invaluable for drawing strength during those moments of vulnerability. In my case, I was blessed with an incredibly supportive partner who provided comfort and assurance along every step— even through times of despair when there seemed no end in sight.

Utilizing the experiences and knowledge of others can be a powerful tool in propelling us forward. When we come from an open, humble place not only are those around willing to help, but they often have invaluable advice that wouldn't normally present itself if it weren't for their insight. Learning what has already been done is also key—there's so much grace and wisdom available to greatly benefit our paths ahead. By putting together pieces of advice and wisdom, I slowly gained insight into how to create the best path for myself.

Final Thoughts

The road less traveled is never an easy one, but it has been the most rewarding journey I have ever taken. Along the way, I have learned more about myself and my place in this world than I could have ever imagined. Stepping out of our comfort zone and blazing new trails can be a fulfilling experience—let's all embrace the journey!

CHAPTER FIVE

THE ART OF INCLUSIVE LEADERSHIP

*"If history has taught us anything, it's
that we ought to pay attention when
certain voices are excluded."*

Angella Mignon-Smith, P.Eng

www.stemhubfoundation.com

Ig: @angella_means_messenger
Fb: @Angella Mignon-Smith
Li: @Angella Mignon-Smith, P.Eng
T: @ms_mignon
Goodreads: @Angella Mignon-Smith

Angella Mignon-Smith, P.Eng

Angella Mignon-Smith is an engineer, volunteer, and lifelong learner. Born in Winnipeg, Manitoba, she's an experienced public speaker who has appeared at over a dozen events and is currently serving as the Board President of STEMHub Foundation, a charity focused on bringing high-quality Science, Technology, Engineering & Mathematics (STEM) programs to underserved communities in the greater Toronto area. Angella is dedicated not only to giving back but also to showing her two daughters the importance of education and the possibility of taking a less traditional path. Angella is the daughter of immigrants and is very interested in history, social justice, personal finance, and health and wellness. She's a strong believer that education and business are the keys to advancing the Black community. Angella believes that sponsorship and allyship is necessary to help advance women in the workforce. When she's not researching stocks and cryptocurrencies, you can find her training for her next distance race with a Charlotte-based running club called Madmiles.

I knew instinctively when I met Steve that I'd come to learn his story; I had this odd way of making people feel comfortable enough in my presence to share. When we met, I found it curious that a polished, tall, dark, handsome, and seemingly educated middle-aged man was working in the setting he was in. After a few conversations, Steve shared the reason why.

Steve had been excited to start his first proper job in Canada some years prior, moving his family to a small rural town to start a job at a manufacturing company named Kapston. As a foreigner and person of color, he knew the move would be a big adjustment, especially for his wife and their two children. But Steve had finally landed a job in his field of choice, accounting, after completing both an undergraduate degree and a master's degree. After a rigorous interview process, they selected him to be a manager in Kapston's finance department.

Steve told me what a great experience he had in his new role at first. He enjoyed his work, got along well with his immediate boss, and had the opportunity to utilize his specialized accounting skills to add value to the organization. However, that positive first year would be short-lived. Life for Steve took a dramatic turn when his boss left the company and he had to report to a superior he did not know. Steve sensed his new boss was uneasy with his attempts at relationship-building, and he noticed his work environment growing more and more toxic despite his attempts to remain cordial with his new manager. The toxicity infected his direct reports as well; work he'd counted on his staff to complete wasn't getting finished on time or was incomplete at best. At times, Steve found himself having to pick up the slack for his staff who hadn't completed their tasks. Steve didn't want to admit it was bigotry and xenophobia he was experiencing because, after all, his first year at the company had been excellent. But the discord and negativity persisted.

After months of these conditions, Steve finally mustered up the courage to approach HR about the ongoing issues with his staff and about how his boss treated him. HR promised they would look into the matter, but the situation persisted; soon Steve fell into a depression and ended up taking leave. The entire ordeal had taken a huge toll on Steve's mental well-being, and he was literally exhausted. The final straw that pushed Steve to turn in his resignation came when he learned HR had included his manager on their initial call without Steve's knowledge. He had expected his call with them to be in confidence and he felt hurt, betrayed, frustrated, and most of all disrespected.

After Steve left Kapston, he learned he wasn't alone in his experience. It turned out that other minority staff had experienced similar treatment and also left the organization. In a disheartening end of his story, Steve was now working in a field that no longer drew upon his expertise in the financial industry. His dream career was now a memory, and he found himself working in a completely different sector, in a role that was relatively entry level despite his advanced degrees. I suspect the change also left Steve with a reduction in pay, which meant a change in lifestyle for his family. Steve's family remained supportive and were able to adapt, however, and Steve no longer faced bigotry in his current role. At least to my eyes, he appeared content.

While Steve's name and place of employment has been changed, this story is based on true events. Here's an interesting perspective: Steve is a Black male working in a Science, Technology, Engineering & Math (STEM) field. He is a man in a predominantly male environment. If this happened to Steve with only race being a factor, the next logical question becomes, "How do similar experiences affect Black women, or other women of color?" Research suggests that Black women are more likely to face discrimination in the workplace; forty percent of Black women in the U.S. say they need to provide more evidence of their competence compared to fourteen percent of men.[1] Pew Research

---

1   "Lean In, Working at the Intersection: What Black women are up against," Lean In, accessed December 2022, https://leanin.org/black-women-racism-discrimination-at-work.

found in a U.S. survey that sixty-two percent of Blacks in STEM say they have faced racial/ethnic discrimination.[2] While these types of statistic aren't available in Canada, it is a harrowing indicator of how rampant discrimination is in the workforce culture.

We hear consistent stories of women, especially women of color, being "The Only": the only person in a particular category (i.e., Black person or woman) in a workplace setting, in a meeting, at a certain level of an organization, etc. "The Only" means you are immediately recognized and potentially marginalized. While some would suggest that this could help you stand out, it also carries the expectation that you won't fit in either, and that feeling is lonely. Such a scenario is not at all uncommon. It can be seen in both my and my contemporaries' experiences of bringing advanced degrees and knowledge to a job only to not be paid as much as our superiors, even those who do not possess the same education, knowledge, or experience. This inequity often persists to the point when the BIPOC (Black, Indigenous, and people of color) individual feels like they will never be promoted. I've also been privy to instances when racism and sexism in the workplace were left unaddressed despite being raised to HR, much like Steve's story. The BIPOC women involved in these instances grew tired and ended up leaving the companies in question, despite their talent, education, and experience.

These stories form just a subset of what I believe to be a larger group of stories about what it's like to be Black in a corporate setting. In the examples I've provided, it didn't matter whether the Black person was Canadian-born or a foreigner either. I, too, have experienced this "othering" both in my academic experiences and during my career. One experience I recall vividly came in my second year of university. I was studying at the engineering building one day when I spotted one of my professors. We acknowledged each other with our eyes, and he kept on with his business. Then he turned and approached me, as if to start a conversation. I perked up, ready to hear what he had to say, only

2   C. Funk and K. Parker, "Blacks in STEM jobs are especially concerned about diversity and discrimination in the workplace," Pew Research Center, January 9, 2018, https://www.pewresearch.org/social-trends/2018/01/09/blacks-in-stem-jobs-are-especially-concerned-about-diversity-and-discrimination-in-the-workplace/

to be met with a curt, "Are you pregnant?" I recall how humiliated I felt at that moment, and how grateful I was that the group I was studying with did not hear my professor's inquiry. In complete shock that I'd been asked such an invasive question, I could only barely stammer out the word, "No." I walked away completely humiliated, while my professor walked away with a nonchalant air I will never forget in my life. Would the question have been asked of me if I were one of the handful of white female students in his class? Perhaps my professor was eccentric, a jerk, or plain old sexist; I didn't know him well enough to know his intentions, but this did not negate the inappropriateness of the encounter or the feeling it gave me of being an outsider.

Such experiences are nothing new to us as BIPOC individuals. It's the tax of working in a corporate and sometimes even an academic setting. There is a feeling of paying a tariff simply for being the outlier culture in professional settings. We know tokenism, microaggressions, feeling overlooked and not included in important conversations about work and career progression. Worse yet, we know those situations when our ideas aren't acknowledged in a group (meeting) setting, but as soon as they come from someone else, they are readily accepted. We feel the pressure of needing to conform to fit in, leaving behind our cultures, parts of our identities, or our musical tastes and sometimes even changing ourselves (hair styles, styles of speech) in order to not only "make it" but to advance. We know what it feels like to be told, "You are not really Black" or "You speak well." I personally have chosen simply not to discuss racial injustice in corporate spaces because I've been told, "They should have complied" when yet another unarmed Black person is gunned down by police.

Being "The Only" can be downright exhausting because often we are gaslighted when we explain our feelings to others. In more extreme instances, BIPOC individuals can have their emotional displays in cross-racial settings hijacked by non-BIPOC individuals, as depicted in Robin Diangelo's ground-breaking book White Fragility.[3] The emotional toll of these experiences leaves Blacks and other minorities feeling unsupported, not included, and in

---

3   R. Diangelo, *White Fragility* (New York: Beacon Press, 2018).

the worst instances, disrespected to the point of considering alternative employment. So it really is no surprise that Black women in the U.S.[4] and Indigenous women in Canada[5] are the fastest growing demographics of entrepreneurs. This data suggests the BIPOC community is creating our own corporate settings with their own cultures.

There has been a noticeable shift in corporate Canada recently. More diversified workforces have been shown to outperform their less diverse competitors, as conveyed in McKinsey's well-publicized "Diversity Matters" study.[6] The Harvard Business Review has also provided data to support McKinsey's research. "EBIT (a term for operating margins expressed as per sale basis after accounting for variable costs but before paying any interest or taxes margins) for companies with diverse management teams was nearly 10% higher than for companies with below-average management diversity."[7]

In addition, Diversity and Inclusion (D&I) initiatives have sprung up in many organizations across the STEM fields and beyond. There were over 4,000 open Diversity and Inclusion Director positions posted on LinkedIn in the U.S. alone at the time of this writing. This shows promise that our society is championing action to diversify corporate boards and advance women. Canadian universities are now pushing harder to increase the number of female engineering students enrolled in their programs, with the University of Toronto achieving forty percent female first year enrollment as of 2017.[8] Corporations like Toronto Dominion

4   R. Umoh, "Black Women Among The Fastest-Growing Entrepreneurs – Then Covid Arrived," Forbes, October 26, 2020, https://www.forbes.com/sites/ruthumoh/2020/10/26/black-women-were-among-the-fastest-growing-entrepreneurs-then-covid-arrived/?sh=278aee656e01.

5   Ibid.

6   S. Levine, "Diversity Confirmed To Boost Innovation and Financial Results," Forbes, January 15, 2020, https://www.forbes.com/sites/forbesinsights/2020/01/15/diversity-confirmed-to-boost-innovation-and-financial-results/?sh=44038fc9c4a6.

7   Ibid.

8   R. Baker, "Increasing diversity, inclusivity lead priorities of a new Academic Plan," University of Toronto, November 17, 2017, https://news.engineering.utoronto.ca/increasing-diversity-inclusivity-lead-priorities-of-new-academic-plan/.

Bank, the Royal Bank of Canada, Firmex, and BenchSci have given back to initiatives to support disenfranchised communities, as I've witnessed through my own volunteer board work with a charity called STEMHub Foundation. I'm truly grateful to know and be a part of something that will hopefully make the future a little brighter (and hopefully easier) for my two daughters. But it is important that inaction does not waste the momentum of these opportunities. All levels of society need to accept that people of color, and more specifically women, deserve a seat at the table.

Diversity isn't the final destination. It isn't enough to have token BIPOC or female individuals in leadership roles within our organizations. It isn't enough to put out flowery corporate social media statements the next time police kill another unarmed Black man. Rainbow corporate banners come June are simply hot air if the organization and its leadership isn't truly invested in inclusion.

Further cultural shifts are required, and time is needed to see this through. These shifts cannot be temporary, quick blitz actions that are just swept under the rug until the next social travesty involving a Black person happens. Inclusive cultures need to become a societal norm, and this will require consistent and sustained effort across not only all tiers of an organization but of our society. Once we get there, BIPOC will no longer need to be identified as "The Only" but will instead become "One Of."

Inclusion is the framework needed to transform our organizations, and action today will leverage future generations to even greater heights. Organizational leadership must lead the charge.

What does this idea of inclusive leadership really mean? First and foremost, a leader needs to create an environment of respect, where people feel seen, heard, and valued. When my previous manager approached me to join his new project, he knew I had very little background in the field; however, I'd made it known to him I was always willing to learn something new. He enthusiastically came by my cube one day and said he wanted me to work on his project, along with another junior engineer. He assured me I would learn a lot and said it would be a very technically challenging project. I was nervous, but it felt good to be trusted with high-profile work. At no point did he ever micromanage any of the members of our team. In fact, he almost had a hands-off attitude from the very beginning. That was simply his way of approaching leadership: creating an environment of respect and trust.

Being a woman of color in a male-dominated field can sometimes leave you feeling like you need to keep aspects of your life private, including family life and your role as a caregiver. I've never wanted to give the impression that my children are a scapegoat for why I could not perform at my best at any task I was given. However, I also felt leery of taking time off work for my daughters' appointments and events. Sometimes I'd be ambiguous when requesting absences from work. Thankfully, my boss was always understanding and would even reassure me that my family commitments came before the project. There were even a few times I requested time off because of my D&I involvement, and my requests were met with understanding and praise.

My work in D&I allowed me to learn about another McKinsey study called "Women Matter – The Present and Future of Women at work in Canada"[9] regarding advancing women in the workforce. This study found that women are still much more likely to provide caretaking roles to children and elderly family members. We are also more likely to be doing most of the housework within the home even though many of us have partners and careers. In essence, Women need flexibility; it then becomes incumbent on our managers and leaders to understand which caregiver roles we are responsible for when we are not in the office and to provide that flexibility if and when it is required. Flexibility also involves office scheduling as well. It isn't necessarily convenient to hold meetings in the later hours of the day or expect that we will respond to an email sent late in the evening or on a Saturday right away. The pandemic and the fact that as many as one-third of employable Canadians have worked from home doesn't

---

9   D. Amato, "Indigenous Entrepreneurship in Canada: The Impact and the Opportunity," RBC Royal Bank Online, June 18, 2020, https://discover. rbcroyalbank.com/indigenous-entrepreneurship-in-canada-the-impact-and-the-opportunity/.

magically make these off-hour emails and late day meetings easier or more inclusive for women either, as discussed in "How the Best Bosses Interrupt Bias on their Teams."[10]

It's sad to me that we have hashtags to depict our experiences as Black women. The hashtag I find the most troubling is #believeblackwomen. Despite us being the most educated demographic according to U.S. data, we still need this hashtag in various aspects of life, from our medical care and mortality prospects to the live birth rates for our children and the rate at which we die in childbirth despite socio-economic factors being removed. These statistics all attest to the fact that Black women are typically not believed when we speak up, whether that be about our pain, how we are treated in the workplace, or even when we experience violence and abuse. It isn't just Black women either. According to "How the Best Bosses Interrupt Bias on their Teams," women are much more likely to be spoken over even in something as simple as a meeting setting: a testament to others not believing us or giving weight to what we say. I have not been immune to this and have seen it happen in action.

What action can leaders and allies take if they witness this behavior happening to women in their teams? Allies should most definitely speak up. They can simply say something like, "I believe Angella mentioned that in our meeting last week, and it was a great idea." Leaders should also ensure that everyone invited to a meeting has had an opportunity to speak. Sometimes introverts or more quiet people tend to stay away from voicing concerns, but if someone in a position of authority encourages active participation, it could help bring out ideas. I experienced this in a meeting that involved others outside of my regular project group. I was particularly quiet, and the manager in this case was gracious enough to ask, "Angella, do you have anything to add to the discussion?" I appreciated being given the opportunity to contribute, and the manager's behavior left an impression on me and others in the room.

---

10   J.C. Williams and S. Mihaylo, "How the Best Bosses Interrupt Bias on Their Teams," Harvard Business Review, November 2019, https://hbr-org.cdn. ampproject.org/c/s/hbr.org/amp/2019/11/how-the-best-bosses-interrupt-bias-on-their-teams.

My journey on social media has led me to predominately Black-led spaces. Facebook in particular has many groups geared toward ethnic minorities. Each of these groups has its own administration, and rules for entry require that you identify with said ethnic group. A common theme I find in some of these spaces for Black women is a self-imposed requirement for excellence. Many Black people, especially Black women, are raised with the mindset of striving to achieve "Black Excellence." My own mother told me at a young age, "We have to work twice as hard to be seen as half as good." I believe the fact that Black women are so highly educated yet are paid a fraction of what their white male counterparts doing the exact same role make is a direct reflection of this belief.[11] This push to continually excel without actually being rewarded in the workforce is discouraging.

Worse yet, if/when we actually make a misstep, we can be met with harsh criticism. What can leaders do to support BIPOC individuals when things don't go as planned? In my most recent project, the team faced many issues early on. Some of them had to do with the original estimates for the job, while others, I admit, lay with my own inexperience on the subject matter, not to mention my health struggles behind closed doors. My mistake caused a setback on the project, and I was open with my manager and supervisor about my situation. Instead of receiving harsh reprimand, my manager was understanding. He compassionately yet professionally gave me a warning not to repeat my mistake and to ensure I got my project back on track. I was grateful to him, and his reaction fueled me to work harder (both at the job and on repairing my health). I naturally wanted to do a good job for someone I felt looked out for and respected me and my humanity.

"While it might sound like an excuse, the unfortunate reality is that there is a very limited pool of black [sic] talent to recruit from." This was a quote from Wells Fargo CEO Charles Scharf in a recent article I saw posted on LinkedIn.[12] The comments

11 V. Hunt, D. Layton, and S. Prince, S., "Diversity Matters," McKinsey Online, February 2, 2015, https://www.mckinsey.com/insights/organization/~/media/2497d4ae4b534ee89d929cc6e3aea485.ashx.

12 "Wells Fargo CEO's Comments about Diverse Talent Anger Some Employees," CNBC Online, September 22, 2020, https://www.cnbc.com/2020/09/22/wells-fargo-ceo-ruffles-feathers-with-comments-about-

under the article left me with a sentiment of disgust. I find it truly hard to believe that despite certain female demographics being the top in both education and entrepreneurship there are simply not enough BIPOC individuals to diversify any board setting. At the heart of this issue lies two things: access and networks. Many BIPOC individuals simply do not have access to large networks. At the completion of my engineering degree, it took me over a year to find a job. I finished my degree with honors, won an academic bursary after my third year, came in first in my group student paper competition in my fourth year, and completed a thirteen-month internship. I had no relatives at a manufacturing facility who could help me get my foot in any door and initially had to work in a completely unrelated field with a much lower starting salary to make ends meet. If corporations are truly serious about diversifying their top ranks, then they will need to be the ones to do the looking.

Another thing leaders have to do is sponsor and mentor women and BIPOC individuals, inside and outside of their own organizations. After I'd been appointed STEMHub's board president, the role provided me with a line of sight to all aspects of the organization. I'm confident the events of 2020 have led to an increase in partnerships and donations. Two of STEMHub's most high-profile partnerships are with Toronto-based tech companies called BenchSci and Firmex; STEMHub has joined forces with them to create a mentorship program that allows volunteer employees to provide mentorship to BIPOC youth. The CEO of Firmex personally volunteers his time to provide mentorship to some of STEMHub's BIPOC leaders. My hope is that through these bonds, some of STEMHub's charity board members will sit on corporate boards in the future. Within my own company, mentorship and dedicated programs support diversity initiatives and new hires. Intentional allyship is required to dismantle homogeneity and foster diversity at every level.

We all have a vision in our mind of what a good leader looks like. I'm fairly confident that the meme I've read the most on LinkedIn is, "People don't leave bad workplaces, they leave bad bosses." This quote really takes me back to my previous manager.

diverse-talent.html.

I always had a sense of belonging in my group when working with him. He never spoke down to me, he provided me with opportunities to learn and grow, he always encouraged me to use my voice, and he provided me with the flexibility I needed to have a life outside of his project. I didn't feel apprehension about being a female / Black working for him at any point, ever. Even when I did mess up, his reaction fueled me to work harder at the job. I think leaders need to take a good hard look in the mirror at how they truly treat their own reports, and organizations need to understand and dig deeper into why BIPOC / women leave. If attempts are at all made to uncover the true root cause of attrition, especially if it's happening more frequently within the minority groups, I'm convinced that it would be clear that it's inclusion that is the real issue; because at the core of inclusion is respect.

CHAPTER SIX

LET GO

*"Do not allow your own perceptions of
the world, or other people's perceptions
of you, to drive the direction of your life.
Instead, use them as an opportunity to
draw on your personal power and build
on your strengths, even the ones you
don't recognize at the moment."*

Michelle H. El Khoury, PhD

www.yogamazia.com
ig: @yogamazia
fb: @yogamazia
li: www.linkedin.com/in/elkhourymichelle
t: @yogamazia

Michelle H. El Khoury, PhD

Michelle H. El Khoury, PhD is a wellness entrepreneur and former pharmaceutical executive with over twenty years of healthcare experience. Her journey, coupled with her background and passion for yoga, led her to open Yogamazia, a yoga studio dedicated to pregnant persons, children, and families. Michelle uses yoga as a doorway for discussions on race, gender, and other social inequities to help empower the future generation of leaders. She believes that yoga is a powerful vehicle for creating a fairer and more equal world and aspires for students to understand the practice holistically—not just through the postures that many believe are its basis but also through its moral and social teachings. Michelle believes women and children are vital ambassadors for change, and she is grateful to serve as a global ambassador for Yoga Gives Back. She is also a health and wellness educator with Integrative Health at Children's Health of Philadelphia. She holds a BSc in pharmacy, MS in health sciences in clinical research administration, and a PhD in public health, epidemiology; she has authored several peer-reviewed research articles, published in medical journals, and presented at conferences. Michelle is a wife and a mom to three daughters and resides just outside of Philadelphia, Pennsylvania.

"HERE, EVERY CREED AND RACE FIND AN EQUAL PLACE."

These words are from the National Anthem of Trinidad and Tobago, the birth country in which I was raised. Like many others of West Indian heritage, my background is a mixing pot; our numerous racial, ethnic, and religious groups are linked to every continent on Earth. Race or a person's skin color did not play a predominant role in conversations when I was growing up the way it does now that I live in the United States. Growing up, I also assumed that all genders were considered equal. It was not until I entered the corporate sector that I realized that there was more to be done to these factors; this realization would lead me to want to fight for a better world for my daughters and all future women of color.

It's surprising that I did not find yoga earlier in my life, but I realize now that it was meant to find me exactly when it did—at thirty-six years old in the first trimester of pregnancy with my second daughter. Little did I know then that eight months later, not only would I have a newborn but I would also uproot my life and relocate halfway around the world. At that time, I was at what most would consider the height of my career. I was a Director in the pharmaceutical industry, a level that took me eleven years to attain compared to other colleagues with similar education and/or much less experience. I was at a crossroads, questioning my journey in life, having to weigh continuing my climb up the corporate ladder with supporting my spouse's career. Looking back, I realize that was the start of a journey to finding my true life purpose.

Perception vs. Reality

There is a perception that education is key to a better life. I was one of the first in my family's generation, along with a few cousins, to graduate from university. I financed my graduate degrees on my own while working full time and enduring no sleep. I completed the dissertation for my doctorate in the aftermath of a divorce while raising my first daughter on my own. There were many days of both mental and financial struggles.

Now don't get me wrong—while I advocate for the importance of higher education, it may not necessarily lead to a life that is better. This depends on how you define "better." I landed my first job at one of the top ten pharma companies in the world, and a few short years into practicing pharmacy, I was so excited that I did not even think there was a need to negotiate my salary. I clearly had not received "the memo" and would definitely have benefited from Minda Harts' book[1] had it been published seventeen years earlier. It did not take long before the reality of the world started kicking in. I learned that one of my white counterparts with the same education, experience, job role, and level made a significantly higher salary than me. This colleague also seemed to have better relationships with the managers and senior leaders and was trusted with more senior tasks for our level at the time. I was also one of no more than ten persons of color in the department; I won't mention the denominator. And while my experience at that company gave me lifelong friendships, it also paved the way for the wage gaps I continued to observe throughout my career. Not much has changed in terms of diversity since then; in fact, like other industries, the disparity within the pharma industry grows significantly with increasing levels of leadership.

Being an educated woman also did/does not exclude me from experiencing microaggressions, both personally and professionally. These include things like being ignored by white clerks while shopping, being mistaken for the clerk by white customers,

---

1   M. Harts, The Memo: What Women of Color Need to Know to Secure a Seat at the Table (New York: Seal Press, 2019).

being asked to confirm home ownership at my doorstep, or being asked if I am mother to my children (because their skin color is lighter than mine).

These microaggressions do not go away in the corporate world, and being educated does not mean that you will receive the same level of respect as your white or male peers. If ever there was a way to take away your pride in moments of your career, hearing words like "You're so lucky" after a promotion would do it. As though my combined years of education, experience, and hard work did not play a role. And this isn't even talking about the blatant lack of acknowledgement by those who feel threatened by this combination in a woman of color. Although my career gave me the opportunity to forge relationships with many "key opinion leaders" in academia, it did not preclude me from experiencing their narcissistic behavior. There also seem to be no limits when it comes to the invasion of privacy of women of color in the workplace, or to the expectations of behavior thrown our way that are most likely not set for our white or male colleagues.

As excruciating as some of those moments were, each one allowed me to shape the reality of the world that I wanted, not only for myself but also for my daughters and for others. Do not allow your own perceptions of the world, or other people's perceptions of you, to drive the direction of your life. Instead, use them as an opportunity to draw on your personal power and build on your strengths, even the ones you don't recognize at the moment. Create your own reality, one that ensures respect for yourself, but do it with respect for others as well. Direct those strengths to others looking to you for guidance, whether it be (your) children, students, family, friends, coworkers, colleagues who you supervise, or your neighbors. Trust in your ability to help others avoid the negative paths you rode on.

With time, I grew comfortable using my leadership roles not only as an opportunity to initiate or further conversations on disparities in the workplace but also to provide support for women and persons of color. To this day, every promotion I received in my corporate career, with the exception of one, was provided to me by a person of color. Each of those persons believed in the worth of their employees, irrespective of their gender or race, and supported them based on their developmental goals, providing honest direction rather than taking a "playbook approach" and ignoring the political backlash. Never underestimate how far you can go when you have the support you need, and never hesitate to return the favor.

Yogi in the Desert

I was introduced to yoga while sitting at a local YMCA waiting for my daughter and (second) husband to complete a karate class. I remember asking myself whether it was possible to have a different birth experience and turning around to see a yoga class next door. Now, social media might have you thinking that you can only do yoga if you are white, female, slim, and as bendy as a pretzel. And although that was true for that particular class, I felt brave enough to ask the teacher whether I could join since I was four months pregnant. She asked me, "Are you breathing?", to which I answered affirmatively with a slightly confused look on my face. "Then you're already practicing yoga," she responded.

Yoga was the calm I needed after the storm of losses we had recently experienced. Apart from the many disparate social and racial determinants of health, research continues to demonstrate that African Americans remain the least healthy ethnic group in the U.S. (Office of Minority Health Resource Center[2]). As of 2020, maternal mortality rates (the number of maternal deaths per 100,000 live births) for non-Hispanic Black women was 2.9 times higher than the rate for non-Hispanic White women (National Center for Health Statistics[3]).

I am grateful to have been able to afford the care I was provided during my second pregnancy, supplemented by yoga instructors who taught that the practice was not about the asanas or poses but about using our breath to bring more awareness to

[2] "Health Disparities Bibliography," U.S. Department of Health and Human Services Office of Minority Health, last modified July 1, 2021, https://www. minorityhealth.hhs.gov/omh/browse.aspx?lvl=3&lvlid=102.

[3] D. L. Hoyert, "Maternal Mortality Rates in the United States, 2020," Center for Disease Control, 2022, https://www.cdc.gov/nchs/data/hestat/maternal-mortality/2020/E-stat-Maternal-Mortality-Rates-2022.pdf.

ourselves through mind and body. Although I was not fully in-corporating yoga into my life then, it didn't take long to notice the positive mental and physical effects it had, especially during delivery and later on with my children after they were introduced to it.

During that pregnancy, my husband was presented with an opportunity that would give him experience to further advance his career. The catch? We would have to relocate to the city of Dubai in the United Arab Emirates. As enticing as that might sound to you, this was one of the most difficult decisions I had to make in my life. It was already a handful to balance a career with motherhood; now having to balance motherhood and ca-reer growth in a new country presented a whole new set of chal-lenges. To make matters worse, upon presenting the situation to my leadership at the time, I was told that I would need to resign from my current role and take my chances at finding a new op-portunity with a partnering company upon relocation. Eventual-ly, after considering all factors and three months after my second daughter was born, we relocated to Dubai, where we lived for the next three years. During the first half of that time, I took a break from the corporate world.

It was during this break that I began to delve more into my yoga practice and completed my yoga teacher training courses. Yoga became an integral part of my parallel journeys of becoming more one with myself and motherhood, supporting my husband, and also realizing my career goals and finding more meaning in my life.

My yoga journey soon shifted from me trying to ease my labor and delivery to my children running onto my mat when I rolled it out or coming to sit next to me while I was in meditation, without a sound and just happy to be in the moment together. In other words, it became solidified as a practice that was less about just breathing or poses and more about a way of life. When I was pregnant with my third daughter, I incorporated hypno-birthing techniques and was able to have a mindful, completely pain-free, and safe home birth delivery. I attribute my increased breathing and meditation practices to my ability to hold myself together then and later on during other difficult moments in my corporate career.

What I mostly remember about this period was a deep sense of gratitude. I went from having remorse for having to give up my job and pause my career to accepting that it was much easier for my husband, and white men in general, to attain their goals. I was grateful for the time this experience abroad provided me to be with my girls and to reshape my path and the many opportunities it provided. I was also happy that I was able to delve more into my yogic path, from the teachers to the students and friendships. My children were able to experience one of the most diverse cultures in the world, and we were able to travel to countries we may not have considered had we not lived in Dubai. And my home birth experience awakened a part of me that wanted to help other pregnant persons embrace their bodies and get more out of their own birth plans.

During the midst of this crossroads in my corporate career and growth in my family, I began to contemplate my life's path. BIPOC representation unfortunately continues to be limited in yoga, sometimes without regard to the practice's East Indian ethnic roots. I had been teaching yoga privately but two months post-delivery, I felt pressured to return to the corporate world. One year later we moved back to the United States.

But this time, it was different. I made a promise that I would not allow myself to become so absorbed in my career that I forgot what mattered most. I wanted to better show up for my children because I knew they were watching. Little did I know the change this desire would lead to years later, not just for my daughters but for other women and children as well.

Yoga and Motherhood

Two years after moving back home, as I continued to climb the corporate ladder, manage various teams in different parts of the world, and travel frequently, I was hospitalized for an irregular heart rate. I was also starting to feel mentally drained. As much as I loved my job, I was being subjected to workplace harassment and did not have the support I needed, at home or at work, to help me overcome what felt like hell at the time.

As I lay in the hospital bed, I asked myself, "Is this it?" Was I supposed to accept my life as it was? I was discharged with strict cardiologist monitoring and had to wear a portable heart monitor twenty-four/seven, and to make matters worse, my temporary medical absence was used to further instigate actions that almost led me to quit upon my return to work. If it had not been for the support of honest human beings who truly knew me and my work ethic, I would have. Burnout is real. Anxiety and depression are real. No matter what phase of life you're in, they can appear. I was again faced with having to reconsider my life's path.

I realized that I could not perform as a mother, wife, and leader if I was not focusing on my own self-care. As Maya Angelou said, "If you're always trying to be normal, you will never know how amazing you can be." We cannot demonstrate how amazing we women can be by checking off all the regular boxes just because that is how it was done in the past. We need to write our own HERstory and to do that, we need to choose ourselves first, finding self-acceptance and making ourselves a priority. I finally started to realize that I needed to be the best me before I could even be good for anyone or at anything else.

Yoga continued to help shape how I wanted to take care of myself, beyond the benefits it gave me during/post-pregnancy. I was more motivated to deepen and improve upon my practice. I restarted using visualizations and affirming mantra techniques. Having more time to focus spiritually, reflect on my beliefs, and appreciate my mind-body connection on a daily basis created an inexplicable, overwhelming aura. I began to feel a shift in how I approached certain aspects of my life and how I handled adversity, both personally and professionally. My deepening practice allowed me to better understand my true purpose, hold space, and show up for others who needed me.

Trying to balance motherhood amongst everything else was exhausting, and it still is! However, I no longer strive to be the perfect mother, or wife, or person. Instead I use my yoga practice to keep empowering myself and teach my daughters, future women of color, the confidence they need to be able to battle the social challenges they now experience and to speak up for themselves in a way that I never did.

I've also learned that taking care of ourselves while balancing all of our other roles in life isn't something we can, or should, do alone. Connecting with other "mothers" who can support you mentally, emotionally, and physically is extremely important. They are the part of your tribe who would drop what they're doing and hold space for you, no questions asked. And remember, a mother is not just someone who gives life with a womb, but someone who gives life with their love. It could be a sister, friend, colleague, or even a stranger in some cases.

Live in G.R.A.C.E.

When I decided to leave my career in pharma to become an entrepreneur, I did not expect the prejudices I experienced in my corporate life to stop. In fact, I was able to better identify and address the racism, genderism, and gaslighting that my white (especially female) entrepreneur colleagues do not experience. I also view this as an opportunity to educate them on our differences and how they can better support women and people of color in the workplace.

Since the COVID-19 pandemic, the number of active Black-owned, Asian-owned, and Latinx-owned businesses has declined between twenty-five and forty-one percent, compared to a twenty-one-percent decline for the general population (National Bureau of Economic Research[4]). A recent CBS News Money[5] segment reported that Black-owned businesses were twice as likely to fail during the pandemic. Why is that? Why aren't white-owned businesses as likely to fail?

If two entrepreneurs walked into a bank, one Black woman

---

4   R. Fairlie, "COVID-19, Small Business Owners, and Racial Inequality. National Bureau of Economic Research, 2020, https://www.nber.org/reporter/2020number4/covid-19-small-business-owners-and-racial-inequality.
5   "Black-owned businesses twice as likely to fail during pandemic," CBS News Online, August 5, 2020, https://www.cbsnews.com/news/black-owned-businesses-twice-as-likely-to-fail-during-pandemic/.

starting a yoga business and one white man wanting to purchase properties for real estate investment, each with top-notch credit scores, six-figure savings, sound financial assets, and solid small business plans, would they not have the same odds of being approved for a loan and receiving subsequent support in their various industries? The unfortunate answer is no (putting aside the pandemic, and using the same example to contrast with a white woman). I eventually bootstrapped my business because it was "not considered a good investment."

My (white) husband and I were also the poster children for what the gender wage gap looks like in corporate America. He consistently earned more than me annually (despite having similar education and experience as me and working in the same industry), while I was just supposed to be happy and grateful for my promotions (and I was). He, and my white colleagues, could never understand how this type of bias truly makes people of color feel because they do not experience it directly.

But I draw upon the words of my very good friend, Camelia "Mimi" Felton, who always reminds me: "Don't compare yourself to others, compare yourself to the person from yesterday." So I felt my feelings by finding a channel for my emotions. You can do this, too. Laugh, cry, shout, pray, journal, sing, dance, but always breathe. Keep breathing. Let go of any energy that draws attention away from yourself so that your mind stays in the present moment, focused on all of the good that you need to do. This will allow you to continue being the change maker you already are.

Over the years, as I saw how yoga helped me to cope with my own stress, I also began to observe how it could help my children as well. Rates of anxiety and depression in kids have doubled since the COVID pandemic,[6] but they were already headed that way even pre-pandemic. In 2018, research showed that 7.7% of kids aged three to seventeen years in the United States had been diagnosed with an anxiety disorder[7]—that's about 4.4 million

---

6   B.A. McArthur, J.E. Cooke, R. Eirich, J. Zhu, and S. Madigan, "Global Prevalence of Depressive and Anxiety Symptoms in Children and Adolescents During COVID-19: A Meta-analysis," JAMA Pediatrics, 175(11), 1142–1150.

7   "Anxiety and depression in children: Get the facts," Centers for Disease Control and Prevention (CDC), 2021, https://www.cdc.gov/

children! Suicide is also a leading cause of death among youth.[8] However, research also shows that yoga and mindfulness are effective in improving anxiety symptoms in children.[9]

It was my journey as a pharmacist, published researcher, and corporate executive that led and inspired me to empower other women and children to push the roadblocks placed in front of us that move us further away from equality and inclusivity. With my corporate experience and utilizing my yoga training, I formed Yogamazia. Yogamazia serves as a sanctuary for expectant persons and children to realize their inherent peace through the practice of yoga and the embodiment of its values of G.R.A.C.E.— gratitude, respect, authenticity, community, and equity.

Yoga philosophy teaches us to be true to ourselves, both on and off the mat. If we live by this ethic, it would mean living in our satya, or truth, and believing in something bigger than ourselves. I finally got to this point by saying two words to myself over and over: Let go. When you let go, you release the perceptions of unfairness or injustices, the expectations people have placed on you in the past, and what you believe is expected of you now. You also open yourself up to start again, connect more closely with your inner self, and find the courage to fight for what you believe in.

Don't ever feel the need to defend your divine feminine power. Instead claim it and embrace your inner Goddess, no matter how it shows up. Trust your intuition and connect to your true self, speaking or chanting positive words to yourself frequently so that you can find healing and balance in all aspects of your life. You deserve this life. You are worthy and you are needed in this world. Once you learn to love and believe in yourself, then you can radiate that love and energy to those around you, and that will pay itself forward.

---

childrensmentalhealth/features/anxiety-depression-children.html.

8   World Health Organization (WHO). (2021). "Suicide key facts," World Health Organization (WHO), 2022, https://www.who.int/news-room/fact-sheets/detail/suicide#:~:text=Suicide%20occurs%20throughout%20the%20lifespan,all%20regions%20of%20the%20world.

9   A. James-Palmer, E.Z. Anderson, L. Zucker, et al. "Yoga as an Intervention for the Reduction of Symptoms of Anxiety and Depression in Children and Adolescents: A Systematic Review," Frontiers in Pediatrics, 8 (2021), 78.

And while discussions on gender, race, and other inequities may continue for quite some time, their history is not lost. Ensuring that we, including children, are empowered to be who we are and who we want to be, irrespective of factors like race or sexuality or gender or social status, is just one step toward human equality. So women of color: let go, live in G.R.A.C.E., and rise!

CHAPTER SEVEN

DISPELLING DARKNESS

"My experiences reflect darkness as impermanent, with light lending light at every juncture. I believe we need to own, share, and be the light for ourselves and for each other at every opportunity."

Dana Christina Williams

ig: @christina_williams_author
fb: @christina.williams.author
li: @christina-williams-4370266
t: @CJWILLIAMS13
Goodreads: @danachristinawilliams

Amazon Author: @dana.christina.williams

Dana Christina Williams

Christina Williams is the grateful and blessed mother of two beautiful daughters, Maya and Edie, and wife to the love of her life, Robert, an international lacrosse leader. Residing in the greater Vancouver area in British Columbia, Christina has over twenty years' experience in the marketing, media, and advertising fields and is also a graduate of Cornell University's Diversity and Inclusion program. Christina is a devoted volunteer in her community and dedicates her time and energy in helping to provide a safe and happy environment for children and youth, most specifically young women. The daughter of a fierce, strong, and loving mother, and patient, loving and dependable step father, Christina is committed to driving positive change for all women with every opportunity. As a BIPOC woman in full support of forward movement, Christina believes that our honest, vulnerable voices and written words can be a powerful drive for change. She endeavors to continue to amplify her experiences to lend light toward the paths of other women.

BIRTH

I was born Dana Christina Jarvie in Richmond Hill, Ontario in 1976, to Pam, my strong, determined, and dedicated then-seventeen-year-old mother and my predominantly absent, teenage father. We lived in Ontario for a short time and then relocated as a family to Vancouver where we lived until I was about two years old. Shared recollections from my mother and family frame our early years in Vancouver as challenging, but being resolute, Mom managed to bear the storms of my biological father to keep me safe, happy, and strong. The weight of this relationship found us moving from Vancouver to Trail, British Columbia without him around 1978, where I spent the next seventeen years growing up.

Nestled in the Kootenays, Trail is a beautiful, small, close-knit community full of great families, including mine. Being biracial (Mom is white and my biological father was black) in a predominantly all-white community and growing up within an all-white family, I always knew I was unique, but I had no real narrative about how the color of my skin may place me into tough arenas as I grew up. Mom has always been a testament to the belief that with hard work, internal strength, and belief in one's self, dreams come true. She led through experience, and I have witnessed her successfully surmount all challenges in her life to ultimately change the trajectory of mine, connecting me with the first real father I've ever had and with him making my childhood wish come true by giving me my beautiful brother, Shane, and sister, Shauna, as well. Mom personified the idea that when life knocks you down, you get back up, every single time.

Here I will share with you a few of my tougher life experiences, during which my personal light has had to bend itself through darkness to ultimately shine through.

Big Decision, Little Girl

"Is today the day?"

I ask myself this question often as I approach a certain corner on my walk home as a little girl.

"Should I go to the right, down the alley today or stay on the street, where will the monster be hiding?"

The decision itself is a very very big one as I have no way of knowing if the huge white dog will be tied up out front or out back. This dog terrorizes my youth with its menacing bark, sharp teeth, and angry eyes; it hates me and makes it clear it wants a piece of me every chance it gets. Crossing the street is not an option on my walks home as Funky John's (the community strip club) is on the other side of the street and I am not permitted to walk there or I will face trouble and / or certain hell from "him" at home.

This dog is huge, especially to skinny, bony little me, and this part of my walk is always a tough part of my day.

The day the dog and I had our first real interaction is a day I'll never forget. I remember it like it is still happening. I am at the juncture when I have to determine my path past its home—the back alley or front street—and decide that the back alley is going to be my best bet. I heft my backpack tightly to my shoulders, look down at my scabby brown knees, take a deep breath, and start to walk. I make it about six houses down the back alley, almost tip-toeing, hoping for some type of neighborhood whisper that would confirm that the dog is out front and I'm safe . . .but today is not that day. I approach the house, too afraid to look directly, and see out of the corner of my eye two large ears rising together, coupled with a deep, menacing, guttural growl. Long claws scratch along cement as the beast clamors to gain its footing, and then he's running for me and I'm in that slow motion state, frozen before something awful is about to happen. I realize that not only is the dog out back, he's not tied up at all, and today is the day I'll die. I do the only thing I can in split seconds. I drop my bag and sprint directly up the hood and onto the roof of a shiny blue sports car that has just pulled into the alley. The dog tries to follow, but the driver (clearly having no fear of ferocious beasts at all) shoos

92

him off and cries/pleads for me to come down off of his roof. I do not. I sit resolutely on top of his roof until he actually drives me to the end and out of the alley. As I am sitting on the roof contemplating how I just faced death, I feel a shift. I decide that I will not put myself into a position to fear this animal ever again. I decide at that moment that I would rather brave Funky John's head-on and subsequently face any of "his" consequences at home. Light shining through a moment of darkness.

Consequences

I am an active kid with a vivid imagination. I know I can be anything I want with hard work and determination, and I spend much time considering what I want to be in life. Mom works three jobs to make ends meet for us; as such, I am often home with "him," a professional drinker with a monstrous temper and crushingly heavy hands. I love him very much and as a little girl consider him my father; it is through my experiences with him that I realize I could make it a career as a hair spinner in the circus. These ladies hang suspended from their hair and spin and spin and spin, making it look effortless. I always marvel at them, knowing deep down that I could do that, too. He taught me to do this at home, with some key differences. Instead of the fancy outfits, he suspends me by my hair naked while repeatedly whipping my tiny back/backside with his sharp leather belt, eventually having to change the venue from my bedroom to the bathroom so it will be easier to clean up my uncontrolled defecations afterwards.

My skinny frame aches at school as I sit on the hard chair at my desk. I often have to make a note to check my body for a few weeks after a whipping to mark the progress of my shrinking bruises before deciding whether sweatpants would be the necessary attire for my next gymnastics practice. He prepares me with stories to tell if anyone should notice, but I don't speak of it with anyone, including my family, assuming that they all must know. I do very well in sports and have learned early on that I have great balance and am fast, strong, and nimble. I enjoy gymnastics, swimming, skating, running, basically any sport I could do that gives me a reprieve from time spent with him and the opportunity to be in "trouble." I make the most of my season passes for skating and the community pool over and over, often walking to the rink or the pool in the morning with a bagged lunch and staying all day long, until hopefully Mom is home. When they speak about physical abuse at school or on TV in the afterschool specials, a small bell rings in my head but almost inaudibly. It can't be happening to me; surely other kids are disciplined like this at home; after all, how did the actual hair spinners figure out they were good at it? If this is in fact happening only to me, I never want the embarrassment of my peers knowing or to do anything to embarrass or hurt my family. I resort to telling myself to do everything I can to stay out of the way and be a good girl—which ultimately proves impossible as I never stay out of trouble with him for long.

Decision Day

I feel a shift on the day I realize that his goal with these whippings is to terrify me and make me cry, that he gets something out of hurting and scaring me. With that shift, I realize that I know his worst and recognize that I believe I can manage it. The next time he snaps his belt at me to let me know what is coming and shuts the door so his monster can bear no witness, I hold the air in the room when he attempts to steal it. An internal resolve grows where the usual itchy tendril of fear that flops around my stomach before a whipping usually begins. It rises up my back and across my collar bones to rest firmly under my chin; I can still feel it as I write it here. It is almost as if I feel myself grow bigger as little me looks directly into his eyes. The familiar tremble and cower from my end is gone, replaced with my eye contact, silence and resolution. When he suspends and spins me by my hair while whipping me that day, I am silent and find his eyes with every opportunity. I discover very quickly and surprisingly that I mollify the monster. My whippings stop from that day onward. It evolves to me sitting in my room repeating, "I'm going to be a good girl" over and over and over and over, but he never whips me again. A burst of light from inside in an otherwise dark moment that changes everything. Mom ultimately leaves him and then sets us on our path to the brighter days just over the horizon.

Young Woman of Color

Our Black community in Trail was very small. Most of the children in the other Black families were younger than me, save one family with a girl very close to my age. We were great friends in elementary school, and I identified with her in a way that to me felt familial, sisterly. Her mom and her brother were lovely, and I remember wishing that her mom would braid my hair in the microbraids she did so well on my friend. Her mom would sit in their kitchen cooking plantain bananas with a beautiful scarf around her hair, and I was just fascinated by the whole experience. This early friend and her family helped shape my first real identification as a woman of color, and I am very grateful for my experiences with them. I've always felt a bit at a loss for knowing very little about my Black family and have always wished for a deeper sense of my black history.

I had the privilege of growing up with really beautiful friends, many of whom I still cherish and am friends with today. My first best friend was a boy named Shane whom I met in preschool and stayed close to through life, along with my friends Sheila, Sara, and Catharine. My experiences have shown that good friends offer a resilience to carry us through anything and provide footing when it feels like the bottom of the world might fall out. These special people have been the calm in many of my life's storms, and I recognize that I've been lucky to have them on more than one occasion . . .

"You're an Ugly Fucking Nigger"

During adolescence, color rarely came up in my close inner circles, but the few times it did, it was visceral. Our town was small, and all of the children had predominantly come up together. By grade ten, I felt I had grown into myself and had finally fully embraced my big, curly brown hair. I felt safe and comfortable in my community, surrounded by my loving family and friends. I loved sports, school, and my after school jobs and was overall an affable teenager who got along with and liked just about everyone. Living life like this, my first experience with racism hit me like a puncture wound, leaving in its wake an unfillable hole.

Grade ten math class. Whispers, hard to discern until I recognize they are not only there but directed at me. I find the source and look up to be met with the surprisingly cold and hateful glare of a boy I had grown up with since elementary school. "Hey Christina, you are an ugly fucking nigger. I'm going to beat the shit out of you, you ugly fucking nigger," he whispers, over and over and over. I can still feel the immediate shock, panic, and that old tendril of fear flopping around in the pit of my stomach as his barrage continued. With no tools with which to respond, I sit there scared, at a loss for what to do. I simply freeze, feeling paused in purgatory as a large part of my innocence is stolen. I immediately go from feeling happy and safe to victimized and scared.

Then the shift: I find a light through the dark. I look around for help and spot my buddy Shane. He sits very close to me in class, and I instinctively call out his name to get his attention. Shane is a cool, well-liked guy and also a fighter. In seconds, I instinctively recognize him as my potential solace in this situation. I know he won't let anything happen to me, I'd grown up with him like a brother, so I simply (and shakingly) say, "I need to talk to you right after class," just loud enough for the newly announced racist beside me to hear. That, thankfully, is literally all I need to do to stop the attack coming from beside me and move forward. That boy never bothers me again, and I have no other memories of him until he reaches out to me on social media to be "friends" twenty-five years later. I decline.

I don't actually know if Shane knows how integral he was to me at that moment in my life, but I'll never forget the day that I was grateful to have borrowed his light to illuminate and dispel racism, a newfound, ugly, and scary darkness. I learned that day that simply reaching out in a time of need can have an immediate, positive effect on a dark situation.

Nigger, Again

Grade twelve. I am at a celebratory track-and-field team dinner at the beginning of my grad year, and the conversation turns to the upcoming student council election. I loosely mention that I might run for grad president (haven't really considered it but am definitely open to the idea) and at the end of the evening, one of my teammates tells me that a girl on our team is upset about my potential campaigning.

The next day, late for school, I am surprised to find one of my friends waiting for me at my locker, warning me to not trust anyone and telling me she needs to speak to me at break. She is surprisingly, visibly angry, and I wonder what could be going on. The hallways have cleared as I make my way to my first class. I turn a corner and find myself in the hallway with the girl who had reportedly been upset at dinner the night before. She grabs my hands forcing me to stop moving and says, "Christina, I have never called you a dumb nigger."

Shock . . . I reply, "Okay . . . ?" and continue to walk to class. She calls after me, "Don't you want to talk about this?" to which I reply, "No," trying unsuccessfully to simply erase the moment from my mind.

At break, I learn that this girl had in fact told a group of mutual friends that morning that "no nigger would win grad president over her." My blinders fall off, replaced with a clear vision and a seething rage. I feel as if I'm outside of my body as the world gets quiet and I cover (again in perceived slow motion) the expanse of the school over to the fieldhouse where I know she'll be standing. I rumble over to her, an earthquake inside, and with absolute resolution say, "If you ever look at, breathe on, or speak my name again, I'll beat the fucking shit out of you." My finger trembling in her face. I have never fought or even touched a person in anger before, but at that moment, I feel like I could throw her over the school.

A long, drawn-out melee ensues, involving teachers, school counselors (I am a peer counselor at that time), and our families. I ask to be signed out of school early that day as I don't feel I have the proper tools to manage or respond to the situation; I had thought that this girl was my friend. I get my backpack from my locker and start to trudge toward the exit doors, carrying what feels like the weight of the school. I am in shock as I realize that there are for sure others who feel the same way about me. It feels as if my safe and close-knit community has evaporated. There are others. Why had I let my guard down after the grade ten incident? I realize that I had been naive to assume that was an isolated incident when clearly racism is a position shared in predominantly disguised communality.

This circular narrative runs a painful, isolating marathon through my mind. A bell rings as I make my way toward the exit and the halls fill with students. I have my eyes glued to the ground, feeling vulnerable, embarrassed and painfully exposed, when a set of feet stops directly in front of mine, very intentionally halting me in the hallway traffic. With angst and trepidation, my eyes travel up the person's body to rest on the eyes of a very kind, smart, and sweet girl from our school. She reaches out both of her hands, takes mine and smiles."Good for you, Christina," she emanates, with light, "Good for you" and then she walks on. Her warmth is powerful and pierces extreme light and warmth toward me through that heavy moment of darkness.

After a long night of reflection, I go to school the next day, and the first thing I do is submit my intent to campaign for grad president. This is less an intent to win and more a campaign for me to show up for myself (and my community). I have decided that I will not shrink nor cower under the weight of racism. On speech day, I stand tall in front of my peers, my voice and speech paper shaking, and I represent myself. It is terrifying but my spark gives me strength and I do it.

Do I win? No. The presidency goes to the most deserving student, one who leads our class impeccably through our final year. But do I WIN? Yes. I win by showing up for myself, my peers, and my community. Following the election and through our grad year, there is a visceral show of support for me amongst our peers that helps me to move through the experience to have a wonderful grad year. However, I can't help but notice that my adversary's experience may not exactly mirror mine.

That summer, after our school year ends, I am at the local drive-in movie one night and see the girl there. We gravitate toward each other in the dark until we stand facing each other. Silent seconds pass as we look at each other, and then she apologizes. We embrace and I forgive her before parting ways.

Looking back I learned from that experience that just as light lends light, dark can lend dark reciprocally. I believe that we both suffered through ignorance and ultimately grew together through forgiveness.

Adulthood

Analyzing some of the shadowy moments of my life has revealed that there has also always been an external light pushing through these experiences towards me. While I've been growing internally and finding ways to find and manage my spark while shining and bending my light through my life's challenges, an infinite glow has also been magnetically drawing through, helping to dispel the darkness from the outside.

I have a deep appreciation for my blessings. For example, I started my life with an abusive father figure and was subsequently blessed to know and rely on the safety of paternal love through my relationship with my stepfather, Cyril. My relationship with my late father-in-law Rick was incredibly special as well, blessing our family with a stoic, paternal love that was relied upon perpetually. This love lives on through my soulmate: my thoughtful, loving, and supportive husband, Robert.

The women in my life have predominantly been formidable and kind with my mother, the matriarch, leading the way. Pam harnesses her warrior instincts with class, kindness, and an open heart that has shown through example that we can get through absolutely anything and do it with love. My mother-in-law Linda offers a unique gift to our family as well. Outside of having created the greatest man I've ever known, she's led with a fierce love that has crumbled any obstacle for her family.

Robert and I are both proud members of the BIPOC community, (Roberts family has strong lines into the Tlingit, Metis and Japanese communities) and we admire and honor the light of our parents/family/ancestors before us by endeavoring to lead our girls with the same fractals of honesty, vulnerability, and love. We are committed and diligent in raising our girls, Maya and Edie, with pride for their combined heritages and we support and encourage them to challenge everything. They are strong, smart, kind and beautiful girls, already independently cognizant of underlying, derogatory societal cues that they show no fear in challenging. Honoring challenges and carrying the light of our families through to our babies is a legacy we feel proud and privileged to continue.

There are many movements I am part of through a combination of experience and chosen position. Power, I believe, emanates through openness, adaptability, and in the sharing of experience. One of many favorite quotes is: "Speak your truth, even if your voice shakes" encapsulating the importance of sharing to empower and support others to find safety in their experiences and do the same.

To you, reader, thank you so much for allowing me to share some of my life's more challenging moments with you. I hope my words might inspire you in tough times to find the courage to trust and project your light while drawing in the warmth coming to you from just over your horizon.

CHAPTER EIGHT

FROM ELISION TO POWER

"Power is not an external construct; it is an embodied sense.

The feminine divine beholding herself with grace,

stretching far back and far forward through generations of time."

Gina Wong

https://ginawongsite.wixsite.com/ginawong
https://asiangoldribbon.com/

ig: @trree_asianmom_psychologist
fb: @TRREEofLifeLeadershipLegacy
li: @gina-wong-71429051
Goodreads: @drginawong

Gina Wong

Gina Wong has always been a lover of stories and words. During undergrad, she bought herself a card that said, "Someday you will write a book." She completed her Ph.D. in Counselling Psychology at the UofA and is a licensed psychologist in Alberta, Canada. As a best-selling author, she has published four books and has been a professor for twenty years. In addition to counseling racialized women, she specializes in maternal mental health forensics and initiated the Postpartum Support International Canada. She finds most fulfillment in her clinical practice providing counseling, workshops, and consultation to individuals and groups. Gina is a social justice advocate and an engaged speaker at national and international levels. She developed the TRREE of Life, Leadership, and Legacy™ counseling model and is the founder and chairperson of the Asian Gold Ribbon campaign. She received the 2022 Canadian Counselling and Psychotherapy Leadership Award and the 2022 Psychologist of the Year Award (Alberta) for her work in racial justice and perinatal mental health. She is grateful for her loving parents, three sisters, and extended family. Gina currently lives in Alberta in her home with TB. Together, they have a son and two daughters, and a lot of pets.

I bolt. Hurl myself into four lanes of traffic. Instinct catapults legs to action. No thought. Growling dog lurching at me, pulse racing. Six-year-old panic drains my face; my sisters and I on our way to school. I jettison to escape . . . into screeching cars, blaring horns, and shouts. I once heard that dogs smell fear and that makes you even greater prey for a vicious attack. Terrified, I dart into danger to ward off peril. I run into oncoming traffic, afterwards feeling great shame. Not only stupid, but dangerously so.

In so many ways, this story sums up how I lived my youth and early adult life, and the beliefs I held about myself. Afraid of life, blind-sided by my own fears, turning into danger in ways that served to deepen shame. I ran and hid from my emotions so others wouldn't see me as weak prey. My limbic/nervous system didn't know how to find calm, shelter, or safety. My immigrant parents were themselves trying to survive and find their way by working extremely hard to ensure our family's basic needs, for which I'm indebted. But I had no emotional regulation. Now, as a psychologist and parenting educator, I know emotional co-regulation is foundational to children's ability to learn how to manage their feelings and cope with life; and is integral to their sense of worthiness as adults. Back then, though, my six-year-old self fumbles alone in the dark; without air, without power.

Powerlessness is layered dust.

Stifled, choked, and immoveable.

Powerlessness

The stories I tell are not unique. They are stories of immigrants, their children, minoritized individuals, and any others who have felt the shame of not belonging. Each of us have similar plot lines of pain, commonalities that transcend time and space, and yet each are different . . . needing to be told. Telling "outer-inner battle stories" by creating coherent narratives from fragmented images and memories disarms trauma, as Dr. Dan Siegel, a distinguished clinical professor of psychiatry at UCLA, describes, and is enroute to power.

With no co-regulator for my emotions as a young girl, no safe haven, no protective solace to tether me and silent the raging unknowns, I traversed blindly, filling inner gaps with distraction, giving way to more self-condemnation. Unable to chart myself from a grounded place of worth, I had no compass to safety. Instead, I chose relationships that re-enacted patterns. I behaved in ways, seeking connection and worth, that served to turn me against myself. Twisted up in controlling men's arms to feel some vestige of belonging—even if fleeting. Being as invisible and as small as I could . . . so I could be seen.

Self-elision evolved so naturally for me. As a first-generation Chinese Canadian girl, born in Montreal, I was often the target of anti-Asian hate, though I had no words for it at the time. It felt like I was the most targeted, not my sisters or anyone else, though memories of trauma are fragmented. We were among the few racialized families in our community. I felt alone, trying to defend myself and understand why cruelty from other children was a constant, especially after school.

The cumulation of these experiences at a young age seared a message of "not-good-enough," branded me no matter how much make-up I wore or how many men I could attract as I got older. The beliefs I held about myself had no oxygen to transform. Unworthy was a feather duster, trying to move layered dust accumulated over years, tickling me to submit . . . leaving flecks of dust that dirtied me like that little girl, kicked and shoved in the playground on her way home in grade one. Silent shame is deafening.

I fumbled my way, covering up deep-rooted perceived inadequacies with an outward persona of kind, gentle, pretty, agreeable, not a bother, staying small . . . quiet . . . invisible. Seeking positive attention, white approval, for some measure of worth and value. Filling a cup that would never quench my innermost thirst: deeply dehydrated. Further shamed when my instincts to protect left me all the more vulnerable and wounded. I followed other people's compass, which led me further away from myself. There was no place—only *placeless-ness.*

Rooted Tree

How from these beginnings does a lost soul find itself and its way to power? It starts with connection to community; in my case, connection to other minoritized women who, without words, understand. Power was also forged profoundly by settling into the loving arms of my intimate partner . . . tree-trunks fixed to the earth, bracing me for wear. TB escorts me, boundless in his ability to see me. Holding me constant when all else is ambivalent and amorphous. Without this love, my soul's unrest, the turmoil within, may have been my foregoing calamity. Starting to take stances, voicing my opinions, learning I had them and had a right to them, speaking my mind, no longer that little girl, small and silent; growing comfortable with confrontation and mistakes—all possible because I am tethered. Rooted in mother earth to awaken the feminine divine. Like a wonderland with dreams of possibilities, belonging paved a way for me to connect to myself. The catalyst to roaming free was rootedness. I no longer run amok.

Elision of Asians

For Asian people, an ever-present message of absence is ubiquitous. *Invisible* has been the preferred Asian. The Merriam-Webster dictionary defines elision as "the omission of an unstressed vowel or syllable . . . to achieve a uniform[ity]." Such is the elision of "A" from the BIPOC (Black, Indigenous, Person of Color) acronym. Its absence reflects how Asian people are neither accounted for nor considered in race-conscious dialogue. Naoko Muramatsu and Marshall Chin give voice to the elision of Asian individuals when they write about the categorization of fifty countries with different religions, cultures, and hundreds of languages into one monolithic term "Asian."[1] East, Southeast, and South Asian

---

1   Naoko Muramatsu and Marshall Chin, "Battling Structural Racism

communities in North America, in particular, are stereotyped as the model minority. Racist troupes and erasure translate to neglect of issues faced by Asian people and lead to impoverished culturally responsive resources.[2] Diasporic and North American born Asians are lumped together and then are an inconvenient syllable, not noticed when removed—sometimes even by ourselves . . . like me, who deleted myself for survival.

However, we have entered liminal space. Liminal means to nearly exist. As greater emphasis is placed on the experiences of Asian people, this fosters more legitimacy. I would say my journey to rising in power as an East Asian woman followed this same trajectory. I elided myself (an inconvenient syllable, easily glided over) in an effort to blend in, wishing to be less Chinese, then transformed to liminal existence—allowing parts of my Asian self to surface and am in the process of becoming and growing agency, self-identity, and power in my being.

Stories of Rebellion

Stories of elision and powerlessness were dominant in my girlhood. But in addition, stories I have amassed from shelves of dust are ones of rebellion and spirit, borne through wisdom.

Sparks fly . . . igniting logs. Flame burns and flickers.

Beacon of light from darkness.

I stand as a little Montreal girl looking forward,

and see present spirit rise from the dust. And stand now,

my feminine divine hands reach back to steady

and behold her with grace . . . future self holds all.

She sees us through the light of flickering flame.

One such story is a divergence from what that grade-school

Against Asians in the United States: Call for Public Health to Make the "Invisible" Visible," *Journal of Public Health Management and Practice*, 28, no. 1 (Jan-Feb 2022), https://journals.lww.com/jphmp/fulltext/2022/01001/battling_structural_racism_against_asians_in_the.2.aspx.

2   Ibid.

girl, ridiculed and shamed for being Chinese, understood of herself in youth. The feminine divine now knows and sees warrior tales from old. These are rebellion narratives.

Apart from after school terrorizing, on weekends I somehow transform to girl-rebel. I walk the neighborhood by myself, looking for offending kids to utter slurs or mock me, to press their noses, piglike, and pull at the sides of their eyes. My seven-year-old runs home. Out of breath, I tell my sisters and cousins. All five of us head out, inflamed. Chinese Rat Pack with a mission. I point out the offenders and we shout at them, defend ourselves, and run away.

Tiny fire crackles. A flame emerges from the campfire.

Glowing. Barely bright . . . but offers warmth.

On weekends, I feel proud and protected, vindicated and mischievously rebellious. To this day, I believe I can round the troops and fight back for what is right, fierce with fight against injustices. Staking claim and place.

Power came from powerlessness.

Finding Liminality

A second story of rebellion through pain also stemmed from racial trauma and the tormenting belief that I was bad because of how I looked. Why else would kids spit at me, trip me, and kick me? Racism and hatred turned inward led me to disavow the visible Chinese parts of myself. I stopped speaking in Chinese . . . and dressed and styled myself to fit in with white kids. Elision by others, then myself.

Understandably, my parents see this as an affront to them. They believe I'm ashamed of being Chinese, and of them. I am the black sheep, an outcast. Left on my own without a sense of belonging, I have only myself. I start journaling and writing poetry as an outlet to keep myself company and contain my thoughts through written word (though at the time I didn't know why). My journal entries start with "Dear Gina"—I tell myself about my day and my feelings. I try to make sense of the nonsensical.

Fire feather flames glow bright embers of light.

Flames lick, lighting up the midnight sky.

Little did I know, journalling and poetry were acts of rebellion . . . writing myself and my divine spirit into being, finding liminality.

Leaving to Find Home

My third rebel narrative came in my 30s when inner wisdom whispered very softly, though she was quickly drowned out. When quiet enough, I could sense her. Somewhere in me, an uprising of the divine spirit sounded muted tones and inscribed messages. Finally, translated . . . I knew I needed to leave my marriage for self-preservation.

It was endless pain and anguish in those years, on my own with two young daughters, doing what was best for me in the face of what seemed, to all others, the worst for them. I stood as a bulwark against tyranny. Despite hardship, I made my way with pounding heart. Breathing through the dust.

Log sends bursts of fireworks at once,

licking flames glow brighter and brighter.

Little did I know, this time, the radical act of defiance against social scripts was another howl at the moon, my feminine divine inhabiting . . . noting that pleasing and meeting others' needs chokes oxygen from fire.

Catapult to Action

Through this, a fourth rebellion happened after the March 26, 2021 shooting in Atlanta, Georgia, US. that took the lives of eight people, six of whom were Asian women. This event catapulted me into a life-changing sequela. A path illuminated, beckoning me. I was thrust into news media to represent my experiences and ideas about anti-Asian violence and racism at a time when Sinophobia was being revived. COVID-19 was a cold, hard slap in the face that reawakened pervasive racism, particularly for East

Asians, resurrecting the "yellow peril" stereotype that was created over a hundred years ago to incite disdain and hatred.

This started a processing of the racism I endured earlier in my life and the impact it had on me. I gaze into the eyes of the dirtied girl, fallen down, with scraped knees, covered in layered dust of shame, eclipsed from herself. No longer with despise, I see her for the first time and feel warmth and compassion.

Roaring fire burns bright. Is tended to,

and danced around throughout the night.

Tending to and letting go of inner revolt transmuted into passion to do my part in fighting anti-Asian racism. I envisioned a world that could be different for my daughters, and others, by working to shift belief systems and enhance cultural pride for a new generation of Asian individuals and communities voicing up if they choose, without apology for their authentic selves. I founded the Asian Gold Ribbon (AGR) campaign and started two other organizations that aligned with my passions. I also developed frameworks for the applied practice of cultural safety in academic institutions.

The glow and warmth of the fire burned away long held

limiting beliefs I had about myself.

No longer silent and small, self-elision transformed to

worth and taking up space in my life, and a place in the world.

Power

What I have learned is that power is not a construct. It is an embodied sense. The feminine divine awakening so she may behold herself with grace. A hallowed relationship with myself began, shoring up strength. For me, my current partner, my attachment security and rock (TB) was a foray to self. For others, this could come through any individual who is safe . . . a consistent regulating-other (mentor, coach, friend, family member, therapist, etc.).

My fifth act of rebellion is present day and is only possible through the scaffolding of previous uprisings. It is daunting and undefined. Directly naming and fighting against racial oppression and structural racism in the workplace, I am wayward in my path.

The campfire smoldering,

only a dim beacon of light barely visible.

Somehow I will rise in power.

Midnight sun lightly toasts marshmallow clouds.

The process into my feminine divine, my power, was through storying and restorying trauma, acts of rebellion, writing, reflecting, talking, listening, being creative, meditating, finding mentors and allies, being seen by TB, and above all, growing my relationship with myself. In these processes and connections, I honor my feminine spirit, who is there even in darkness. I garner empathy and compassion for myself, which leads to profound healing. It's a never-ending process that makes me a better person, parent, and psychologist. Like the Russian doll set or matryoshka that sits on my nightstand, each doll is displayed individually, and sometimes nested. A distant future with a strong maternal line, aged through wisdom and grace through generations that start far back and reach far forward. The maternal line is shored, full of love, mutuality, and connection. This is my call to spirit, my work through time.

Stepping Into Her Power

Finding my path to voicing up, in allyship, has fostered deeper cultural connections with myself and others. Coming alive when I founded the Asian Gold Ribbon campaign that engaged 52.3 million this year; more importantly, at the core of my being, I am proud to be Chinese and not ashamed of my past. From the dirtied girl covered in worn dust to my rebel being fighting against anti-Asian racism and toward equity, justice, and inclusivity, my own experiences and inner compass—*my* intuition—compels me.

I also advanced the term BIAPOC to include the A for "Asian/ Desi," instead of using the BIPOC acronym. I prefer the derivative "IBAPOC" [ib-ah-pock], which stands for Indigenous, Black, "Asian/Desi," Persons of Color. "IBAPOC" stands for the need to include Asian people in race-conscious and anti-oppressive dialogue. "IBAPOC" begins to lift us out of invisibility, out from the dusty shadows. This acronym embraces and acknowledges that diasporic Asians have suffered long-standing, individual, and institutionalized violence and racism . . . and that generationally we continue to face these challenges. Erasure provides limited resources, attention, and focus. "IBAPOC" itself is an uprising: an act of rebellion . . . from elision to power.

TRREE of Life, Leadership, and Legacy™

TRREE is based on twenty years of clinical practice and my own journey to power. This framework guides as a conduit for change, focused upon shifting negative intergenerational patterns, proliferating a legacy of power, and engendering future generations. TRREE is a counseling and consulting framework and a life-course approach I specifically developed for racialized women of color, though it is applicable to many. It is grounded in healing-centered engagement (trauma work),[3] relational-cultural theory, attachment theory, and anti-oppressive principles. TRREE focuses upon racialized women's needs and cultivating a life from a place of worthiness.

TRREE is an acronym for a non-linear process involving (1) Trauma (relational and developmental) work, (2) Release of limiting beliefs, (3) nurturance and development of Relationship with self, (4) reducing Ego defenses, and (5) enhancing Emotional regulation. That is, working through inherited generational pain involves healing-centered engagement, releasing limiting beliefs, nurturing our relationship with ourselves, reducing ego defenses, and improving emotional self-regulation. TRREE is to tether to our relationship with ourselves and to embrace imperfections

---

3   Shawn Ginright, "The Future of Healing: Shifting from Trauma Informed Care to Healing Centered Engagement," Medium, May 31, 2018, https:// ginwright.medium.com/the-future-of-healing-shifting-from-trauma-informed-care-to-healing-centered-engagement-634f557ce69c.

through self-compassion, which ultimately fosters compassionate relationships with others.

TRREE is trauma-informed and starts with building coherent narratives around relational trauma and other traumas to give voice to untenable and unnameable feelings. Connecting to our traumas and understanding our neurobiological responses to them, including the need to stay small, leads to recovery. This enables the forging of relationship with self. From a reflective and compassionate self, TRREE also acknowledges ego defenses; that is, how we cope with rejection, criticism, and negativity. It is also through deepening our emotional regulation through co-regulation with another, so that we learn self-regulation, and in turn, be co-regulators to others. Namely, our children.

Processing Trauma through Building Coherent Narratives

As described, a pivotal way to address past trauma in this model is building coherent narratives. No longer avoiding but filling in holes and gaps from traumatic memories lessens the grip they have on us. Mapping our trauma trails, narrating, restorying, and weaving them to a semblance of understanding, while acknowledging emotions that surface, is vital. Dr. Gabor Maté, an eminent Hungarian-Canadian physician specializing in trauma and addiction, also described trauma as a disconnection with self. Indeed, unearthing and reprocessing stories of my youth have been central in claiming inner-power. I trace my battle scars, bloodied and broken-boned. Swallowed up, exiled by others. I understood why I elided myself.

Asian American writer and poet Cathy Park Hong further reinforces the centrality of owning eclipsed parts of ourselves, including emotions with no name. In her book *Minor Feelings: An Asian American's Reckoning*, Hong puts to words the experience of having feelings washed away at sea.[4] She named unnameable feelings, giving me permission to unabashedly recall emotions of shame. There were few words to describe how I felt in my early

---

4   Cathy Park Hong, Minor Feelings: An Asian American Reckoning (New York: One World, 2020).

adulthood when playing games like Trivial Pursuit, where I felt utterly stupid because I didn't know the answers. I believed I was inept when in reality, the game was framed around dominant cultural knowledge. It was not created for racialized minorities with different cultural upbringing. The shame I felt was unacknowledgeable.

Hong also shares that she "always looks sideways at childhood . . . with" side-eyes, telegraphic doubt, suspicion, and ever-contempt," instead of "back at her childhood" like other white adults do."[5] I, too, look sideways at my childhood. I recall one Christmas Eve when I'm nine years old. I carefully hang my sport sock by the fireplace. But no Santa comes. I heard that "stockings were hung by the chimney with care . . ." When nothing happens, I'm confused . . . wondering if it's because I'm bad. In later years, I feel shame and guilt for having expected my parents to do something that they didn't practice; and I feel additional shame because I wanted something other kids had. I felt lesser-than, but didn't know why.

Feelings that were immoveable dust, layered and caked through time, are now validated and normalized by allowing elided, collectively disembodied experiences to be woven together and told. Now I am able to put words to fractured stories of youth.

Recognizing and Reducing Limiting Beliefs

What does staying small, believing, and being guided by fear (limiting beliefs) gain? Naming them, accounting for them, is important. Limiting beliefs are built-in safety nets from rejection, looking stupid, failing, or from being too big or ambitious, which are neurobiological survival strategies. Giving voice to these limiting beliefs, understanding where they came from, and actively facing them with compassion reduces them. They are figments of shame. We have fought Don Quixote's windmills that once upon a time did attack us. But being afraid to take chances, noting our limiting beliefs and holding them to the light with empathy, and taking chances anyway, is to take up space in our own life, with power.

5   Ibid, p. 68.

The heartfire to power lives within a compassionate relationship with ourselves.

Recognizing Ego Defenses

The ego is an integral part of the TRREE framework because understanding our feelings and reactions provides insight. How do we process when we feel important, or known, or loved, and accepted? Having no strong basis for these feelings in childhood, my brain did not know how to compute them. Sometimes I sabotaged things to avoid future inevitable disappointment.

In order to feel worthy, being valued and receiving accolades from others felt like the only way, given that the original source of rejection was from others. Perfectionism and pleasing others were naturally bred as coping and survival needs. Being a human-*doer* instead of human-*being*, as reknowned American professor of medicine Dr. Jon Kabat-Zinn states, or being outcomes/success/achievement focused for worthiness, impedes healthy boundary setting and being responsive to our own needs, which in turn, takes a huge toll on our physical and mental health. Over time, I learned that vulnerability and shared pain resonate with others because perfection and pleasing lead to disconnection with self and others. I came to the conclusion that authentic relationships are what matter the most and are essential to finding inner wisdom of the spirit.

From Elision to Inner Power

Power is bold. Through darkness, it can see the light.

Power is not an entity internalized from the outside. It is not status, nor titles, nor authority. Power is an intimate relationship with self that enables us to sew generational lines together in a way that fosters generosity of spirit and compassion. It acknowledges failures and holds ourselves with grace. Power is not performance toward an achieved outcome. Power is located through storying and through connection that sees us embarking on a journey of self-discovery and belonging. Within this, inner wisdom and power ignite.

Did I perfect how to cultivate power through powerlessness and find presence and agency after invisibility? There are many moments and days when I feel powerful and am connected to inner wisdom and divine self. There are also days when I feel elided, powerless, exhausted, and washed away. Dust settling again. The little Montreal girl with scraped knees bolting into traffic, at times, still hides to be seen. Tethered, I breathe in and out and behold her with love and compassion. I know these days come. The feminine divine patiently makes space. Rooted, I lean into myself and TB and trust the innate wisdom of my future self. Time dimension warping, transcending place. She reaches backward and forward—storying us into being . . . nested, through generations of time.

CHAPTER NINE

EXISTING
WHILE BLACK

"Authenticity is YOUR natural power.
Own. It."

Dionne Bowers

li: https://www.linkedin.com/in/dionne-bowers-fcip-crm-58480323/

Dionne Bowers

Dionne Bowers is a dynamic individual with over twenty years of progressive experience in the insurance industry. She also operates her own consulting business focused on training and development solutions for insurance professionals, and is a contracted facilitator with the Insurance Institute of Canada. Dionne is the co-founder of the Canadian Association of Black Insurance Professionals, a non-profit organization primarily focused on the advancement of Black insurance professionals through advocacy, mentorship, education and networking. She has a strong passion for learning and sharing knowledge with others.

Dionne graduated from the University of Ottawa with a degree in criminology and sociology. She also has a diploma in public and private investigations from Sheridan College and currently holds her Fellowship Chartered Insurance Professional designation, the highest professional designation in Canada's property and casualty industry, as well as her Canadian Risk Management designation.

In her spare time, Dionne enjoys mentoring people and giving back to her community, reading, traveling abroad, the art of boxing (thanks to her best friend), and creating new experiences with family and friends.

Frigid. Fun. Different. These are some of the words that come to mind when I describe growing up in Winnipeg, Manitoba in Canada. Picture this: A young immigrant family of four in the late '70s moving from Kingston, Jamaica, an island riddled with political strife and violence that saw many Jamaicans and their families flee the country they loved, to start over in different parts of the world. My father's near-death experience—staring down the barrel of a gun—convinced my parents to move to a part of Canada that was next-level cold. I mean, there was nothing like it: black flies and a warm summer month or two (depending on the year) that turned into sub-degree cold with a windchill that would make your heart stop. Black ice, snow days from school, snow drifts up to the second-floor window, and listening to my parents describe how the family car had to be plugged in overnight so it could start in the morning. Believe me, when I relive this experience, I am in shock. My younger self often asked why my parents would leave the tropics and go to the tundra. A valid question from a very inquisitive child.

However, despite the weather, Winnipeg had its moments for us young kids. I remember my parents taking us on picnics, going to the zoo, playing baseball, attending cultural events, and making the most of our snow days bundled up in layers upon layers of clothing with Hot Shots in our gloves (I know you are dying with laughter if you know what Hot Shots are). Complete innocence. I am in my late forties as I write this piece, and when I think back on my nine years in Winnipeg, I realize that though it was cold, Winnipeg presented an opportunity for my family to start a new life.

So, why the word "different" to describe my Canadian Prairie experience? I was a year-and-a-half-old when my parents decided it was time to leave Jamaica with two young kids, two suitcases each, and $50 per person in their pockets. I owe everything to them, but they probably didn't realize the extent of the racial injustice that they—or their kids—were about to embark on and endure for the rest of their lives. This is my story.

My dad kept a family photo album with pictures of myself and my three older siblings. I often go through the albums—more so since his passing—to reminisce on the times caught on film: birthday parties in the McDonald's caboose, watching cartoons with my sister, who is two years older, and her friends on snowy mornings, and class photos where often I was one of three Black kids in a class of thirty. Sometimes I was the only one, but there were never more than three of "us." As a youngster, I was somewhat aware that I was not like most of my classmates. I was always the tallest among my peers (both male and female) at school, and I often felt I didn't fit in because of my size and shape.

Growing up, I was extremely conscious of my physical appearance, including the color of my skin, but I was taught that it was "what was on the inside that counted." That belief worked for a while, but when some of my teachers, parents of schoolmates, other students, or even friends started to call me names like "fat nigger," "Black bitch," or just plain old "nigger," it hurt and played a number on the psyche. I am sure some of you reading are in disbelief while others are not, but regardless of what side of the fence you are on, this was my experience during my early childhood, a time when kids should be learning about good versus evil, love versus fear, and right versus wrong. When I reflect on that stage of my life, I think about what my younger self would have appreciated hearing from people other than my parents. Most are words of inspiration like:

1) It's OK to be different. We all have people in our lives whom we look up to and would like to emulate, but do we want to be exactly like them? Absolutely not. We are all unique individuals who have so much to contribute to life. Being dissimilar means having a difference of opinions. It means approaching things from another angle that challenges the status quo. It means giving yourself permission to just be who you were meant to be. The

end. Young people, educators, parents, and other leaders, if there is someone who doesn't look like you, instead of staring at them or calling them names, take the opportunity to learn more about them and embrace who they are and what they stand for. The reality is that people are diverse and it is OK.

2) Speak up. My parents noticed a significant change in my behavior as a result of my experience with racism. I didn't want to go to school, and I was withdrawn at home and unhappy. I didn't feel worthy—a feeling that many children face in society—so I chose to ignore the situation. My parents? Not so much. At a time when I feared the repercussions of speaking up, my parents advocated on my behalf and addressed the issue with educators and parents. The gratitude I have for their actions goes without saying, but it's key for each of us to speak up against any type of injustice that we encounter, regardless of the outcome. In the words of Robert Nesta Marley, "Get up, stand up. Stand up for Your Rights."

3) Believe in yourself. I'm no stranger to adversity and I believe that when you have been affected by it, you build your resiliency; you build your confidence. Children need to know that there are cheerleaders in their corner, elevating them and encouraging them to believe in themselves. Family educators, parents, and those who play a role in child development must be intentional about their commitment to creating a safe and inclusive environment for kids. When we do so, young people develop the self-assurance and skills to make their own way in the world.

A new city meant new beginnings. My father, brother, and family friend set out on a twenty-four-hour road trip east to set up a new home for us. For my dad, the location was convenient for his work; for my mom, it was central enough for her to hop on a bus to get to the train station so that she could get downtown. It appeared to be in a nice enough neighborhood with good schools, which was extremely important for my parents. They wanted more for my siblings and me, and this was their opportunity to provide that for us. Personally, I was excited about this adventure because it meant getting on a plane and finally seeing where we would be living as newcomers to Ontario. What this also meant—and what I wasn't so keen on—was that my sister and I would be starting over: new schools, new friends, new routines. My sister was more of a social butterfly, which was great because it meant that she would lay the foundation for making friends. The recipe for her was to connect with the older siblings and find out if any of them had a younger brother or sister in my grade. This made it so much easier for me because the struggle to make friends was real. I cared deeply about how kids would perceive me and with the number of insecurities I had at the age of ten, I was terrified to put myself out there. Questions that often circulated in my head included things like: What if they don't like me? What if I am the tallest in the class (which was the story of my life from day one)? What if I am the only Black child in the class? All valid questions for children at this key developmental stage, but I had to make sure that I always came back to my parents' words of reassurance. They told me, "Just be yourself," which, in 1986, were difficult words to process. I mean, how do I be myself in this new world that moved at a faster pace of life from the idyllic setting of the Prairies? I can say now, at my age, I am embracing being myself, but at ten years old? Forget it.

My parents always encouraged us to be ourselves, though, so that's what I did my first day of grade five. What I didn't expect was the lukewarm welcome that I received. Yikes! It was like I had been transported to an entirely new universe, one where I didn't belong. I was taller than most, even the boys, but one thing that made me smile was that I was among peers who looked like me. Black.

I walked to the school office hand-in-hand with my father, so he could check me in with the administration staff. Everything seemed so small in comparison to the school that I came from. In my head, with a side order of 'tude (short form for attitude), I thought, "Ontario isn't all that. I can totally do this." Well, five minutes into my first day, I encountered the following:

1) Classmate Number One confronted me and said, without flinching, with her British accent, "My LORD, you're

massive." It's laughable now, and I give her kudos for being so direct, but at the age of ten, I just stood in front of her with a confused look. All I could respond with was, "What?"

2) Classmate Number Two asked where I was from, and I told them I was from Winnipeg. The same classmate then proceeded to tell me I wasn't. Have any of you seen an owl tilt its head? I have mastered that look over the years. I asked the young boy, "What do you mean that I am not from Winnipeg"? He replied with, "I meant where is your family from?" I had to process the question and realized he was asking about my background, so I said, "Jamaica." Then he replied with a resounding, "No, you are not" for the second time. Again, I can find the humor in all of this now, as it has shaped who I am today, but at that point in time, I wanted to go home. It was too much. All I wanted to do was make one friend.

That first day was challenging, I'm not going to lie. The days that followed were riddled with anxiety (on my part) because I didn't know what to expect. There were additional questions from other ten- and eleven-year-old classmates that, in hindsight, were thought provoking but hurt in the moment. Questions like, "What mix are you?" and comments like "...but you're so white" (in response to the color of my skin and how I spoke). They were all statements that stuck with me throughout the years. If I am honest, they were the words that were most damaging.

So, how can you help?

1) In the words of Crosby, Stills, and Nash . . . Teach Your Children (Well). What children absorb in their environments—whether it is at school or at home—is learned behavior. These are the beliefs and actions they will take with them into young adulthood and, if not course-corrected early on, their adult lives. Asking someone what "mix" they are is offensive. Full stop. You mix cake batter with a blender. You mix sand, rock, and gravel to make

cement. You mix gin with tonic after a rough day. Human beings are not mixtures, so do your best to choose your words wisely and carefully.

2) Educate yourself. Read. Observe. Ask questions. Listen. The more you know, the more you grow. "The function of education is to teach one to think intensively and to think critically. Intelligence plus character—this is the goal of true education," Dr. Martin Luther King wisely said. In the 21st century, the world wide web is at our fingertips and there is so much information at our disposal. Educating oneself is so key.

3) Embrace fear. When we fear the unknown, we are often running away from what could be versus sprinting toward something new. Do I have a fear of jumping out of a plane with a parachute? You bet I do, but does it mean that I will never skydive? No, because it is on my bucket list of things to do before I am unable to do so. Do I fear meeting someone who does not look or sound like me? Absolutely not. In fact, I welcome diversity and diversity of thought. Otherwise, how do we grow as a society and enrich our lives if we are in a constant state of sameness? Think about that.

When I was in high school, I found myself struggling to find where I fit in. To the Black/West Indian students, I was too "white," while to the white students, I was definitely "Black." I was caught in the middle of my own internal struggle, with good friends on both sides. Nobody said I had to choose a side, but there were times I felt like an outcast based solely on the color of my skin. This continued into university, where I had one professor of color; while I was surrounded by friends of various ethnicities, my closest friends were white.

I knew in university that I didn't fit the mold. I was very tall, plus-sized, and Black. I embraced my unique self with pride and, for the most part, I got along well with a lot people. I was confident enough to wear high-heeled shoes when I was already six feet tall in bare feet. I was not letting anything diminish my shine . . . until someone would ask me, "What are you?" And just like that, I was the little girl in grade five who was stopped in her tracks, feeling like a circus sideshow. Why can't people be taught to ask about a person's ethnicity instead of asking them "what" they are? It's a question that often made me feel like I was not human, which demonstrates the importance of appropriate language and the need for cultural sensitivity training from an early age.

After my post-secondary education, I started to look for full-time work and was convinced that I would end up in a career in law or law enforcement. I had a vision of becoming a member of the Canadian Security Intelligence Service (CSIS) team at the age of twenty-four, but that didn't materialize because I didn't speak Kurdish (true story). I needed to find something else with a relatively good income, so I could pay off my student debt. My best friend from university, who was working at TD Meloche Monnex at the time, convinced me that the world of insurance was the place to be. Good money, stability, and perks. The idea of selling insurance took some time for me to digest, as I had done everything in my power to stay away from the industry (my father had been a life insurance salesman in Jamaica). However, just like death and taxes, insurance meant job security. It also meant a journey with its own trials and tribulations.

Don't get me wrong: the insurance industry has served me well over the years. There have been many opportunities to learn and experience new challenges, but for some reason, the promotion of Black insurance professionals, never mind a Black female, in a predominately white male industry was—and continues to be—a rarity. The lens that I had to wear meant that no matter how hard I worked, I still had to compromise who I was as a person. I wasn't comfortable doing that, but I did it. It took everything in me to create and be that other persona just to exist, and it was exhausting. When you have been told, "You sound angry" or "Your kind wouldn't understand" in a professional setting with colleagues, at a time when speaking up could jeopardize everything, you find a way to just be. This may resonate with some of you, while others may be in awe and uncomfortable, which is to be expected. Unless these things have been said to you, you can't understand the emotions and trauma that come with being different because of the color of your skin, the texture of your hair, or how you speak ("You're so articulate, Dionne). Twenty-plus years in this industry, and I can say unequivocally that existing while Black in the corporate space is grueling work.

So, where do we go from here?

1) Quit the politics. Imposing one's morals, beliefs, and values on others is something that, outside of the work environment, is often challenged by society. If that is the case, why is the expectation within the workplace that people must conform in order to be accepted and / or promoted? Read that again. Throughout my career, I have been told to "play the game" if I am going to get anywhere in this industry. Why am I playing a game to get to the next level of my career? I have been hired to do a job based on my qualifications, to do the job well, and to excel with hopes of being recognized for my performance. That's it.

2) Create and maintain an environment that fosters inclusivity and encourages individuals to be themselves.

3) Lastly—and most importantly—be intentional in all that you do.

The final two points do not require further explanation because it really is that simple.

CHAPTER TEN

YOUR LIGHT WILL LEAD YOU HOME

"Our greatest trials are what shape us in ways that aren't often seen at first glance. Like an iceberg, what lies beneath the surface is worthy of our attention. Learning to trust our inner light–our knowingness–will always illuminate the path forward."

Lisa Pinnock

ig: lisampinnock
fb: Lisa Pinnock
li: Lisa Pinnock
Goodreads: Lisa Pinnock

Lisa Pinnock

Lisa Pinnock is an educator, musician, writing coach, and lifelong learner. She is a best-selling co-author of *Women, Let's Rise*, an award-winning publication by Golden Brick Road Publishing House.

Lisa loves inspiring women to step into their power and light through community building, advocacy work, and healthy eating with Epicure. Lisa leads a local group of heart-centered entrepreneurial women with FemCity, where she is a global member and facilitates workshops on their platform.

Lisa's involvement as a founding member of Diversity, Equity, and Inclusion Committees with two global organizations has fueled her mission to highlight and amplify the voices of diverse, marginalized communities. She firmly believes that representation matters and that our society is strongest when we embrace the full spectrum of humanity.

Lisa brings decades of combined experience and leadership in a myriad of fields, including music education and performance, classroom teaching, liturgical planning, mentorship, and most recently, lead authoring two new book projects with GBR. She is honored to collaborate with the incredible women who have poured their hearts into writing Volumes One and Two of *Uncover Your Light: Empowering Stories of Hope and Resilience*. Both compilations were published in October 2022 and continue to receive heart-warming reviews from readers across the globe.

So When Are We Going Home?

It was the winter of 1976 when my family emigrated from the warm, breezy climate of island life in Jamaica to what seemed like the polar opposite: a vast, snow-laden, frigid place that I later came to call home. But the process of accepting our new reality didn't happen overnight—not by a long shot! And that's why unpacking these stories has been so meaningful and precious to me, because they've been percolating under the surface for some time now.

For the record, I really and truly thought we were just visiting. In my seven-year-old brain, that's the only thing that made any sense: Mom and Dad brought us here to see our aunts, uncles, and cousins, and then we'd be heading back to Jamaica. I mean, the fact that they bought my brother and me snow gear, enrolled us in the neighborhood school, and moved into a small semi-detached home in Scarborough didn't equate with living here, did it? Not permanently. No, that was just crazy talk! I still remember the night when the penny finally dropped. My mom's sister and her family arrived on our doorstep. We had lived down the street from them in Jamaica, and my three cousins were more like brothers because we were all inseparable. But here they were, magically transplanted to this cold, foreign place just a few months after our arrival. I thought it was odd . . . were they also here for a brief visit? Then I saw the look on my aunt's face as I opened the door. She literally fell into my mother's arms, crying uncontrollably. It was like she had stored up all the feelings about our new reality and poured them out in one long, grief-filled sob. That's when I realized we weren't going back home after all.

The Thing About Change Is That It's Constant

When I reflect on the nature of change, a quote from my third co-authored book, *Uncover Your Light: Empowering Stories of Hope and Resilience* (Volume Two), immediately springs to mind: *"There are times in our lives—upheaval, loss, pain, disappointment—that come about to crack us open, to lay bare the assumptions we hold about ourselves and others. But here's what I've come to learn through some of the darkest moments: They provide opportunities to trust ourselves and the light shining within us."*

Upheaval. Loss. Pain. Disappointment. These were all key players in my family's migration narrative, and each one of us felt their presence in unique and profound ways. With the benefit of hindsight, I can now recognize the impact of these stressors—not in a negative way but rather as the pressure required to turn a piece of coal into a diamond. We can likely all point to a few such pivotal moments in our lives when waves of dormant strength surged from beneath the surface, bringing the brute force of momentum as they crashed onto the shore. And just as water alters the landscape of land and rock in its path, we, too, are changed forever by these meaningful life events.

There were many elements that went into my parents' decision to uproot our entire family to an unknown country. In the political environment in the '70's, there was a looming threat of communism due to the close relations of the Jamaican Prime Minister at the time, Michael Manley, with Fidel Castro. Cuba was only ninety miles from our beautiful island. The seeds of communist ideology were introduced to Manley during his student days at the London School of Economics. He would later bring these concepts to his tenure as Jamaica's Prime Minister, starting in February 1972.

At the same time, the importation of guns emboldened the criminal element on the island, with a consequent increase of violent crime throughout the country. With these factors at play, it's no surprise that a mass exodus began in the 1970's and continued for many years afterward, eroding the fabric of economic stability on the island.

But my parents weren't considering themselves first and foremost in their decision-making back then. Mom and Dad, along with scores of immigrant families, made a series of difficult, sacrificial choices that were exemplary acts of love. They left behind comfortable lives, careers, family and friends, community activities, and numerous intangibles to ensure safety and stability for my brother and me. Although I've said this to them many times before, it bears repeating here: Thank you, Mom and Dad, for *everything*.

Settling into the Unknown

> *"Don't worry 'bout a thing. 'Cause every little thing's gonna be alright."*
>
> -Bob Marley

During the early years of life in Canada, adjustments were being made all around me. My parents made a deliberate effort to shield my brother and me from certain hardships, but a few seeped into my awareness nonetheless. It was a few short years after our arrival that my family made the upward move from a semi-detached place to a fully detached home in the north end of Scarborough. Mom and Dad were so happy about the extra space, along with a large yard that overlooked a ravine. Plus, it was a short walking distance to the local Catholic school. I arrived at St. Ignatius of Loyola in grade six and within days, was being tormented by my classmates for wearing hand-me-downs and not having the latest trendy jeans. And then there was the name-calling: "Paki" was constantly hurled in my direction, but I was completely oblivious to its meaning until years later. At the time, I didn't share these tauntings with my parents or other family members. I could see how hard Mom and Dad were working: teaching piano daily, including weekends, and climbing the corporate ladder at IBM, respectively. I felt they both had enough on their plates without having to deal with my schoolyard drama. Now, with the benefits of hindsight and thirty years of experience as an educator, I would have advised little Lisa to share her burdens and speak her truth. The truth *will* set you free.

I share these painful experiences here for two important reasons, one personal and the other universal. I firmly believe in the healing and transformative powers of writing, both for the author and for the readers who later receive their words. I've had the unique privilege of seeing these concepts play out in real time while working on two co-authored books with thirty-nine incredible (mostly) first-time authors. Our compilations, *Uncover Your Light: Empowering Stories of Hope and Resilience*, provided spaces for these women to unpack and transmute some of their own traumas. It was a beautiful thing to witness, and I'm forever changed as a result. Here's what I've come to learn in recent times: When trauma is unresolved, it takes up residence somewhere in your body until you release it. And writing is one of the most effective, accessible, and cheapest forms of release I can think of.

And now for the universal truth: My family's story is not unique. Not by a long shot. In fact, there are enough immigrant stories out there to easily fill volumes upon volumes. (Note to self: next writing project taking shape!). So often, hardships are viewed as a rite of passage, with an accompanying narrative that places the responsibility for our success or failure solely at our feet. *"You're the ones who decided to come here. Surely you didn't expect it to be easy. No free rides in this country."* And then something about blood, sweat, and tears will inevitably come up. While I may be saying this tongue-in-cheek, there's much validity to flipping this worn-out script to something that sounds more like compassion, kindness, and respect for our fellow humans.

A Brave New World

Did I mention that we moved to Canada in the middle of winter?! Um, yeah . . . still not over it! In addition to adjusting to a very different climate, there were also aspects of culture shock to navigate. And trust me, no guidebook or manual existed at the time. Like so many of life's challenges, it was a learn-as-you-go situation.

This is by no means an exhaustive list, and I'm sure my family members could add even more colorful examples.

- Removing shoes when entering a home in Canada, which wasn't customary in Jamaica.
- Pets being kept in the home. They'd typically be in the yard in Jamaica.
- Addressing co-workers by their first names. In Jamaica, you'd use their title and last name.
- Being asked to contribute a dish to a meal with colleagues or friends. Potluck wasn't a thing in Jamaica, at least not in the years prior to moving here.
- Sayings like *"See you later"* would be confusing to a Jamaican. We'd wonder, *"Am I really seeing you again, so soon?!"*

I recall asking my mom if she could try to dress more like one of our Canadian neighbors. In my desire to fit in, Mrs Cote's outfits seemed way cooler than hers at the time. And for the record, Mom was a very stylish and fashionable lady back home in Jamaica. Writing about it now brings to mind the desperate bids we sometimes make—whether with ourselves or others—to manufacture a sense of belonging. As a newcomer to a foreign land, plus being in the height of puberty, my need for social acceptance was all-encompassing. I share this realization with no self-judgment on board, and certainly many who've been in this position would echo my sentiments. It wasn't until adulthood that I fully appreciated what my parents endured in those early years, straddling two worlds that were disparate on so many levels: culturally, socially, physically, and economically. But they did so with integrity, grace, and bucketfuls of love.

This beautiful compilation you're holding represents my fourth writing adventure in as many years. And each time I'm gifted with these opportunities to reflect and create, I'm amazed at the powerful ways writing can open up pathways for self-discovery and, ultimately, healing. By sharing our stories, we allow space for others to witness their own truths and see themselves reflected back in the words on the page.

So, Dear Reader, what might you glean from these pages that will empower you on your journey? My intention is to help uncover the core values that form the foundation of who *you* are. By identifying and embracing these attributes, you can shine as your brightest and best self, while encouraging others to do the same. In my case, some of the qualities that took root during the formative years of life in a new country were: *compassion*, being *community-oriented, adaptability,* and last but not least, *resilience.*

Within a few short years of moving to Canada, my mom's piano studio became a remarkable hub of musical activity in our neighborhood. Her roster of students kept growing through word-of-mouth, and at one point, she was teaching at lunchtimes, after school, evenings, and weekends. Every dollar earned was welcomed and needed to support our family, but even in light of these circumstances, Mom would regularly offer free lessons to those who couldn't afford them or reduced rates for families with multiple children. What a beautiful example of compassion in action! It has been my experience that being in the underdog position fosters positive characteristics like empathy and compassion. One develops the ability early on to see things from another perspective and, as the saying goes, to walk a mile in someone else's shoes. Bearing witness to the myriad of ways compassion was lived out in the Pinnock household has positively influenced me to this day.

Mom's studio also provided a gateway to the sense of community I was longing for. Her students became some of my best friends, many being new immigrants themselves. It was a place I could be myself, surrounded by like-minded people, and feel wholly accepted and cherished. Our first church, St. Bartholomew's in Scarborough, offered another significant example of belonging for my entire family. We all took on roles in parish life: Mom directed the children's choir, I sang, and my brother, Roger, played the guitar. In later years, Mom passed the torch of directorship to me, and I've been leading church choirs ever since. Meanwhile Dad provided advice, strategies, and budget implementation as the head of the parish's finance committee for several years. When I reflect on his contributions now, I realize he was doing the job of a highly skilled CFO for free. And these are just a few instances of the community-minded work my parents did voluntarily. I remember my brother and I giving up our rooms to put up members of a Jamaican singing group who frequently held concerts in Toronto to raise money for the poor back home. There were never any questions asked, even as teenagers. It was a given that charity began at home and that giving back to those in need was a sacred duty.

The ability to adapt to a variety of situations is a vital part of any species' existence. My belief is that newcomers to a given country need this particular skill in spades in order to survive. Whether it be climate (are you sensing a theme here?!), language, cultural norms, workplace barriers, or social belonging, newcomers are constantly bombarded with situations where adaptation is a must. In fact, these trying experiences are shared by racialized people regardless of their birthplace. As a woman of color, my deepest desire is to equip our young people—our future change makers—with the knowledge that they, too, can rise above any obstacle or challenge they face. I think we can all resonate with the words of the incredible poet and activist, Maya Angelou, in this regard: *"My mission in life is not merely to survive, but to thrive; and to do so with some passion, some compassion, some humor, and some style."* (And that she did.)

And what about resilience? How does that life skill come into play for you, Dear Reader? Through the hills and valleys of the past four years, I've learned that being able to navigate life's storms isn't really about strength. At least, not in the way we often use the term in our society. It's more about knowing your worth and embodying your value, no matter what others may say or do to contradict those facts. It is when we can fully acknowledge our innate beauty and worthiness that resilience becomes amplified in our lives. We can more easily access our intuition and discernment; our interactions and relationships are also enhanced by this knowingness. (Full disclosure: I've always wanted to use the word *knowingness* in some capacity!) I believe that resilience is an attribute whose time has come, in an age when we are being called to look within for guidance and trust the answers we receive.

I'd like to leave you with an effective visualization exercise you can do anytime. I've used this technique with the numerous women I've had the privilege of mentoring through the story-writing process, and my hope is that it'll serve you, too. Inviting you to find somewhere cozy, take a few deep breaths and picture the following scene in your mind's eye. You're speaking in an auditorium filled with engaged listeners. They've all come to hear you share your story; to learn how you got to where you are today and the pathways that led to your success and fulfillment. The emcee introduces you and as she calls your name, the audience erupts into thunderous applause. As you step onto the stage, the bright lights cast a warm glow around you. The moment you've been dreaming about for years has finally arrived! And here's the best part: *you* get to write the script. What will your story—your legacy—look, feel, and sound like? I encourage you to lean into this scene, utilizing all your senses. And if it feels awkward or you're just not sure what words will come, that's okay. Take some time in this present moment, as you read these words, to envision your place in her-story. Then go out and live it, as if it's already done. Sending you much love and light on your journey!

CHAPTER ELEVEN

GIFT-CURSES, LEADERSHIP, BARBIE, AND THE BEAR

"Fishing in bigger ponds: When the world makes you small, crafts a limited story for you—test yourself in another pond. Expand your opportunities, write your own narrative. Be the exception and win on the global stage."

Suzanne M. Duncan

ig: @suzanneduncan1
fb: @suzanne.duncan.790
li: @1suzanneduncan

Suzanne M. Duncan

As managing partner and co-founder of Integrated Sports Solutions, a partner with Toronto's own RISE Integrated Sports & Entertainment, and a co-founder of The Canadian Black Standard, Suzanne Duncan is an award-winning sport marketing maverick possessing the perfect marriage of "off-the chart" EQ and strategic, operational leadership. With over seventeen years in international business relations and sport marketing, the successful orchestration and executions of integrated marketing solutions defined Suzanne's experience for blue-chip global brands. Suzanne has combined her diverse international perspective with a myriad of engagement tactics and story-telling expertise to deliver world class results in the global sport industry. Her stellar leadership is built upon the development and mentorship of high-performance teams within multiple agencies in over four continents across multiple games organizations such as the Olympics, FIFA, NCAA Basketball, Formula One, and the PGA. Suzanne is most proud of her legacy-building work in eliminating barriers to advancement for Black women in marketing through her efforts as a board member and co-founder of The Canadian Black Standard. Though having lived a myriad of the world cities, Suzanne has found home in Toronto, Ontario—a proud bi-racial" Canerican" (Canadian-American).

I was born a leader: not curated over time, not shaped or augmented through a rich career, coaches, mentors, books, self-help, secret habits of successful people, etc. Leadership is in my DNA; I am an old soul with conversations and machinations in my head well beyond my years, for which I have no explanation. Not out of arrogance or conceit do I say this, for I'm baffled myself most times and often expect that others experience this same phenomenon. From what I can recall, it has always been this way. Perhaps others have felt this along their journey and been equally mystified, or perhaps others are far more accepting, even embracing of it. There's an expression that says, "Sometimes the knowing precedes the experience." For me, knowledge and insight preceded a life yet to be lived that was further marked by three distinct moments in my time centered in truth. I call these Genesis, Exodus, and Medved (The Bear).

Genesis

I am a product of a bi-racial, bi-cultural love story, one which demonstrated that acceptance and love are commodities in our society that are not free; they come at a price. My parents were "like souls" in wildly different containers. My mother, an Irish-English Catholic from the American Midwest, and my father, an African-American Baptist from the South. Theirs was a love story anchored in courage and sacrifice. My mother was immediately disowned by her family for her choice of whom to love. My lens as an already curious, self-determined, old-souled five-year-old was forever changed as a result.

As a child, you understand one love: parental, and more specifically, maternal. I recall asking my mommy where her mommy was. She could have shared a veiled, kid-appropriate answer, but she didn't. She simply told me the truth. Her mommy did not like Black people and had disavowed her marriage to my father, and her family had followed suit. So at the age of five, I came to understand the world was not Fisher-Price and Playskool, Barbie, and Cabbage Patch dolls. Love and acceptance were neither genetically prescribed nor guaranteed. Both could be taken away or not even given between a mother and child, let alone anyone else. In discovering "that" was possible, I gained an immediate understanding of the complexities and obstacles that race played in the human experience and what was surely going to be a distinct part of my journey likewise. I wished as a child, as I often do now, that she'd lied to me. I so often don't want to see what I see; I don't want to know what is beyond my understanding for my age and experience or what I myself experience, as so many like myself do, so intensely. I wanted to share in the "privileged bliss" that others experienced before life teaches them otherwise. For the lucky some, "otherwise" never comes.

"Sans choix." As the French say, "No choice." Under the haloed shadow of my two courageous parents, this insight that I possessed was amplified by the special "middle" place that bi-racial children get to feel as they navigate the racial divide. Early on, I could read in between the fine lines of conversations, gestures, rejections bold and subtle from all sides. As bi-racial, fair-skinned people will often attest, there is that in-between that we come to know; it's a lonely place and yet one of privilege likewise because we often unknowingly experience advantages that others do not. And that's only if we are born with fairer skin, finer features, and let's not forget the "good hair." This gift-curse, I call it, allowed me to navigate the landscape and intersections of race, gender, and culture whilst growing up Black, white, Southern, Midwestern, American, and Canadian. No choice but to follow my parents' example in guiding others to participate in society as thought leaders, educators, activists, and game-changers, imagining and crafting a world that was far better than the one we were living in. What they didn't tell me was that all the guidance shared to be twice as good, twice as smart, work twice as hard (the talk we all get), coupled with being a "natural born" leader, was going to be an intensely powerful but often lonely journey.

Exodus

When I was a child, my father went on sabbatical as a visiting professor of social work to Spain and West Africa. He brought our whole family along in an effort to share the global citizenry that was a part of how he viewed the world. I was seven years old and I can recall walking in the narrow entryways of the sand-colored Moroccan Caspar: throngs of children and little fires everywhere for some reason. We came upon a young boy, and my father said, "Do you see him? What do you notice?"

I responded, "He looks like me."

My father followed with, "You're right, and where are you?"

"Morocco." I said matter-of-factly.

He said, "That's right. You're everywhere."

There was an implied consciousness that society was going to define who I was before I had a chance to figure it out on my own. There were boxes with limitations applied by gender and color that were going to be assigned to me, and he wanted to deconstruct that model before it was made. My father and mother understood that if I was to succeed, I would need to measure myself on the global stage—that I was in fact "the world" and nothing less, despite what society had in mind. This exodus from the norm, exodus of thought, had a profound impact on my life. It made the possibilities for the path I would take broad, vast, and limitless. It led me to develop an intrinsically deep fascination with all people and to seek out their cultural mores and their history, to understand how those impact relationships, the workplace, politics, etc. It began my journey and the tagline I often share with others that truly defines my personal and professional legacy: "fishing in bigger ponds." When the world makes you small, crafts a limited story for you—test yourself in another pond. Expand your opportunities, write your own narrative. Be the exception, and win on the global stage.

My first dip into a bigger pond came when I left my hometown Vancouver, British Columbia to attend Spelman College in Atlanta, Georgia. A prestigious historically Black private liberal arts college for African-American women, Spelman was started in the 1800s to educate recently freed women slaves. I wanted to test the impact on education if you removed race and gender from the equation. The "talented tenth," we were called; "the next generation of leaders were being built here," they said. Though even there, I was still "in between the spaces": a bi-racial woman seeking her tribe. Mid-point in university, I met the Ambassador to La Côte D'Ivoire. She was an alumna who shared her journey and what it was like to be an ambassador; it was then I was sold. I would be an ambassador . . . or not. I eventually determined that success as an ambassador would truly only come when I was too old to enjoy it: it would be a stair step and multi-road journey to the top. I recall that the now infamous UN Secretary General Kofi Annan had forty posts before he arrived at that role.

Fast forward a few years and I began my career in sport marketing as an ambassador (of sorts) to the country delegations participating in the Olympic Games in Atlanta, Georgia. My first major professional role started with the engagement of 198 countries of the world, negotiating complex sport issues around participation and qualification. It was then I understood the "You are everywhere" whispered into my ear by my father decades earlier. I would apply for a managerial role in the sport department, successfully completing eight separate interviews in the same day. Sports is a white male over-indexed industry, and I was of course one of the "only ones" in the "Blackest" city in the American South. I felt privileged to be in sport and even more so to be a part of the world's most recognized brand for excellence on the global stage, trusted to be the intermediary between the International Olympic Committee and the delegations of the world.

Русский медведь (The Bear)

From Atlanta to Nagano, Japan to Sydney, Australia, I watched the "movers and shakers" of the "good ol' boys" in the sports space expand their real estate and still managed to carve out a space for myself. There is something to that: examining your spaces, identifying the skills, both soft and hard, of those you're aspiring to be, maximizing your points of distinction, and capitalizing on what sets you apart. Speaking French in the European sport space was my advantage, redefining me as so many were trying to put their finger on my ethnicity. Once whilst sitting in a boardroom overlooking Lac Leman in Lausanne at a table of white men negotiating media rules for sport timing and results, I thought, "How did I get here?" Then a whispered answer: "You're everywhere."

In Nagano, Japan, crouched in a booth with leaders of sport for the Sydney and Japanese Organizing Committees whilst being asked to "take the orders" for all the men at my table, I had the same thought: "How did I get here?" I was watching the eyes of the Japanese hostesses at the same time I participated in business as the only woman in the space. Their eyes were looking at me, awestruck; though it could have been for a variety of reasons, it was partly for sure because I was a Black woman discussing business with a delegation of men—all of us "gaijin" to them. "Fishing in bigger ponds."

That same week in a meeting with IBM Japan, I asked some junior women volunteers in the team what they'd like to do professionally;one young lady shared that she would like to "be like Hillary Clinton" and run for office. The entire room broke out into guffaws. For these women likewise, their narratives pre-written, cultural limitations and gender boxes pre-assigned,

"You're everywhere," he whispered. "Craft your own narrative," he said. "Define yourself and lead by your example," he instructed.

Atlanta, Nagano, Sydney, Salt Lake City, Torino, Beijing, on and on . . . The Olympic torch ruled my professional world as a sport marketer and operationalist. Finally, the Olympics would come to my own pond. I recall thinking, *Finally, I can represent my home team.* I used every tool in my networking toolbox to gain an opportunity with the local organizing committee, by that time sure of being one of the most qualified candidates for a leadership role in the organization. I had written my "Jerry Maguire mission statement" letter to the CEO, John Furlong, about how "I was the embodiment of the Olympics." I shared that I was a Canadian expert coming home to share my wealth of acquired expertise—only to be interviewed by his secretary who had just entered the business of sport. I endured multiple meetings with the fortunate few Caucasian female department leaders, including a human resources vice president who had no experience within the Olympic movement, to assess my intellectual pedigree and professional offerings despite my deep global sport experience. As women of color, we become used to the incessant proving exercises that advance themselves onto us daily in our professions. We get one chance to get it right, one opportunity to prove our intellectual capital, and often only once chance to win! We have normalized the constant scrutiny.

Rejected for a myriad of roles, back to back, I turned my eyes outward once more: "fishing in bigger ponds." I applied with organizations outside of Canada for a role in the Olympics within my own country, my home team, my pond. Determined to achieve my professional goals, I was unrelenting. Perhaps this is where the gift of "knowing preceding the experience" was advantageous. I knew I'd realize my goals regardless of the obstacle because: "You are everywhere," he said. This was my destiny.

I continued to be rejected for multiple roles for eight consecutive years by the Canadian Olympic Committee despite my relationships, experience, and internal referrals. Given the continuity and progress of my career in sport, my qualifications deepened; now the soundbite from female-led leadership post interviews was that I was "overqualified" and "We'd like to give a more junior person a chance to grow in the role."

One of the most significant learnings I can share at this juncture is that the very people who have benefitted the most from diversity, equity, and inclusion stride in industry (sport in particular) have been Caucasian women, in my learned opinion. Contrary to popular belief, it is not Caucasian men who will block your trajectory; it is often white women and other minorities who do so with intention. Given their own fight for a seat at the table that has been denied them likewise, they will rally hard to keep it unless you are significantly well below their rung on that infamous corporate ladder. In this "post-racial reckoning era" with introspective courageous conversations taking place, there has been a slight shift in this trend. A few remarkable Caucasian women and men have stared down their newly identified privilege and are working on transforming their corporate spaces and being true allies for all the "others" previously excluded.Slowly, they are recognizing that intentionality is required, not just the "We hire the most qualified candidate for the role" lie as their benchmark.

After the Vancouver Olympics came London's and Sochi, Russia's. At this juncture in my career, I had been an "only one" for sixteen years; it was a given in the industry I'd chosen and certainly at the level at which I was operating. It is well known that marketing agencies, sport or otherwise, are significantly under-indexed in their diversity efforts. Still, London was a turning point for my "bigger ponds" philosophy. I was representing an American arm of a company in a central London agency. It became clear I was now an "other" for even more reasons and intersects: Woman, race, sport, and culture. This is where the additional "in-between-the-lines" spaces that bi-racial people navigate came in handy, alongside my gift-curse. I could see how to navigate to position myself as a respected leader in short order. Understanding the nuances of British culture and the history that informed it allowed me insights beyond my North American peers. This would lead me to successes supporting the TOP Olympic Partner at that time in one of the most successful campaigns of the most recent Olympic Games sponsorship era: London 2012 Olympics P&G's "Thank you Mom Program." I was now a leader of an award-winning team. In addition, I would be tasked to build on that success by reimagining and reconstructing the same program for the Olympic Winter Games in Sochi, Russia.

Russia is a homogenous, patriarchal society, a former imperialistic empire. Asking a bi-racial Black woman to be the "first" in-country to operationally architect this multi-million dollar sponsorship activation on behalf of a blue chip, global, American brand seemed highly unconventional. Given the American-Russian political climate at the time and Sochi's status as an unknown summer vacation destination on the Black Sea, surely engaging one of the London-based Russian team members would have been more prudent? Needless to say, the whispers of "You are everywhere" dissipated immediately; I may have been everywhere, but I definitely was not there! A non-white, non-male, non-European, non-Russian speaker? Seemingly a recipe for disaster. Loneliness in leadership as "a natural born only" was the least of my challenges.

As someone who played sports through most of my youth and college years, I have lived by the expression, "Champions play hurt." Being uncomfortable is where growth happens, so I was sure there was a lot of growth to be had in my Russian experience. I would travel there weekly whilst living in London. My agency was happy for me to identify the "pain points" for the executive program, to gain fluency in the landscape and the operational planning for the Winter Olympic Games. It was the most difficult and yet self-validating experience I have navigated in my entire career. I called it "Navy Seals training for the brain." This particular area of Russia was unaccustomed to foreigners, as well as to the monster machine that is the Olympics that had landed on their small coastal city. I worked hard to understand the broader Russian culture, the local Armenian-Russian culture, and the Cyrillic alphabet (extremely challenging), as well as to find the middle space between grace and authority: power and authority being the traits most valued in Russia and recognizable in a leader. The Russian Bear symbolizes the might, the power of the post-Soviet era.

I did all of this having no frame of reference, knowledge of the language, or interpreter (which was of course provided to my other colleagues visiting from America).

Moscow was my weekly get-away, and the investment of time in that space proved massively beneficial.I learned that the very asset I used the most—my smile—was interpreted in Russian culture as a symbol of suspicion. I created relationships with men whom I have forever friended as interlocutors who helped me navigate the local civic politics and negotiate with Russian-Armenian Mafia bosses, Kazakh brothel hotel brokers, corrupt regional police chiefs, and FSB (formerly the KGB) officials. I recall being saluted by a local Russian police detail for my leadership and de-escalation skills during an incident involving a conflict between Russian and Ukrainian program guests. My methods to de-escalate this particular situation would never be acceptable in the western world and were epitomized by a dream I had that next night in which my hands had become the paws of the Bear.

Along this solitary journey as the lone operational director in-country and now cultural resource for multiple Olympic partner corporations and our agency, I was notified whilst boarding a flight through Turkey that I'd been passed over for a promotion to vice president, in favor of a Caucasian man. It was a reminder that though I was fishing in bigger ponds, being the big fish still eluded me. A woman had made that choice for my trajectory; I couldn't help but be doubly disturbed that I had challenged myself and delivered big for a corporation, and it was a blonde-haired, blue-eyed woman (an "only" in the senior leadership team herself) who had denied my ascent. I had courageously taken on navigating a new country and challenging culture without any support on behalf of the organization; I was an award-winning and highly recognized leader, but I was not enough to be "the" leader in the end.

My efforts were not in vain, though. I had curated new skills, testing myself as a leader alone as an "only one" in conditions unmatched by any other circumstance in the Western European and North American professional world. I won on the global field of play when failure seemed all but assured. I found a voice without a language to match, connection to a culture that has been relatively isolated (and proudly so), and I how to be a leader; a "Medvev" (The Bear) within one of the toughest political/business constructs in the world. I think ultimately the very gift-curse of as yet "unlived knowing" helped me not only survive but thrive. I recall a soundbite from a client saying, "Suzanne literally pulled some rabbits out of her hat in the Sochi Olympics that no one else could have and that led to our program's overwhelming success."

I am a natural born leader in a container that on the surface appears limiting within this complex, racist, sexist world we were born into—but it doesn't have to be. I've proven it so. It is a gift-curse, this insight that often precedes my lived experience. It is a gift that allows me to negotiate relationships and navigate spaces as an "only one"with fearless tenacity. But it is a curse in that it is often a lonely place, an incessant strategic tightrope walk for what I see first that others don't and that, within this container, demands excellence always. But I have also understood from early on that as women of color, our survival—or, new word, "thrival"—in a racist, misogynist, narcissistic world depends on us playing hurt and championing our own destiny. It requires writing our own narrative and tenaciously overcoming barriers and sometimes even borders that are pre-constructed to limit us. If your pond is too crowded, unyielding in making space for your excellence, remember that you can "fish in bigger ponds," and challenge yourself on the world stage.

Because "you are everywhere."

CHAPTER TWELVE

RISING
POWERFULLY

"Change, progress, and success start by us not sitting on the sidelines. Women of color are the new players, and we are here to upgrade the game."

Lola T. Small

www.lolasmall.com
ig: @lola.t.small
fb: @lolatsmall
li: @lolatsai

Lola T. Small

ola is a Taiwanese-Canadian women's empowerment coach, two-time best-selling and award-winning author, and racial equity advocate. With over twenty-five years of combined experience in children's education, mind-body fitness education, non-profit fundraising, athletic event planning, and empowerment coaching, Lola is passionate about supporting girls and women to share their dreams and impact with the world. A graduate from University of British Columbia in psychology, she is certified in life coaching, health and wellness coaching, and personal training. Lola is the co-founder of Black Lives Rising Media, a social enterprise with education + empowerment programs to raise/amplify powerful Black leaders. Also a Managing Partner of RISE Integrated Sports + Entertainment, Lola shares her expertise in strategic visioning and equitable business development in the world of sports and entertainment.

Through initiatives such as Room to Read, World Pulse, Fem-City, and Black Lives Rising, Lola's work spans Canada, the U.S., Asia, Africa, and the Caribbean.

Lola has published several previous books: *For My Girls, Fitness to Freedom,* and *Women Let's Rise.* She is the lead author for this book project, *We Rise in Power: Amplifying Women of Color and Our Voices for Change.*

Lola currently lives in Burlington, Ontario, Canada with her husband Shawn and their son Jordie.

T he first time I met a white person, I was eleven years old. It would be the beginning of many life-defining events that have brought me to this precise moment in time, and here, in the middle of my fourth decade in life, I am taking on a new purpose and life work, starting with these words.

Life as an immigrant child is intricate before one even sets foot on the new land. There are generations of hopes, fears, and dreams that drive so much pressure and motivation, and the daunting realities of being "the minority" in a new country hit you before you even learn your ABCs. My first brush with racism happened on a mundane shopping day shortly after my family arrived in the U.S. from Taiwan, when a store clerk's cold and demeaning attitude toward my family was so glaringly obvious compared to the kind and warm service she had just given the previous Caucasian customer. My not-yet-fluent-in-English, eleven-year-old self could tell that life as I knew it was about to get very different. A few years later, while we were living in the deep American south, a boy named Michael with an unusually long forehead told me to "go back to where you're from." The only response I could muster at the moment was, "Well . . . *you* go back to where you're from." Such nuances about identity, race relations, and ways to navigate and express our personal power within the layers of society immensely impact how we move through life, especially as a conscious woman of color passionate about the world and humanity.

The quest for racial equity as my focus for social change is fairly new to me, something that was amplified after I married my wonderful husband, a first-generation Canadian of Barbadian descent, and becoming a mom to our incredible son who, at age four, knew that he was Blasian because Daddy is Black and Mommy is Asian. Our family was greatly transformed by the events following the murder of George Floyd in the summer of 2020, and as our four-year-old son marched and chanted "Black

Lives Matter" so loudly that he almost lost his voice, my heightened sense of awareness and responsibility became my new fire. I have always been involved in humanitarian causes and social change projects, mostly focused on girls and women's education and empowerment, but I had never really thought about racial justice. As an Asian woman, I lived my day-to-day white-adjacent and have been lucky enough to not have to endure too many harsh discriminations based on my skin color. We are so steeped in the tea of racism that it took the catalytic events of 2020 to really open my eyes to the realities that others suffer through, including my own talented and loving husband and very likely one day, our beautiful son. Sometimes we are lit up from within to do something for the world, and sometimes the world *commands* us to do something, and my Mama Bear heart heard this deep call. Women of color immersed in the complexities of living life in a racially-layered world are powerful participants in leading the change we need to see for our children. I know of nothing more important or more urgent than to take on work that will shift our world into one that is more just and equitable for all, whether personally, socially, medically, environmentally, and in all arenas of human life.

Start With the Truth of What You Know

I am not a big fan of using the term "minority" to describe myself and other people of color. It feels less-than, not as worthy, and almost like an attempt to continually keep us small. Within myself, I don't feel any of those things. Quite the opposite: I am just as worthy as the next person, I am extremely powerful, and I am here to do important things. In other parts of the world, my race would be the "majority," and certainly the Chinese language I speak dominates all others in terms of numbers. However, since North America internalizes this concept of darker skins being the inferior ones, it's easy to lose yourself and what you know is true within. When the power of words can define the destinies of an entire race of human beings, it's time to reclaim the words we use to represent who we are. The truth within all of us, regardless of skin tone, cultural background, education level, or job title, is that we are tremendously powerful, and our actions affect one another. Each of us has the capacity to share energy, both positive and negative, just by being ourselves. When we can focus on our power to do good, we are the ones moving our world in that direction. It is time to amplify your piece of the action.

I created and self-published my first book in my thirties to empower young girls and to raise funds for girls' education in Asia and Africa through an organization called Room to Read. I love the power of words and books, and I wanted to share that love with girls who may not have others around them to say affirming words to them, much like my childhood growing up in Asia. I also wanted to focus on providing educational opportunities, as I had spent over ten years in children's education and believe in the ability of education to uplift and change girls' lives. I didn't know a single thing about the publishing industry, but my belief and passion in the power of girls made it happen, and it felt like the most natural way for me to make a difference.

Around the same time in my life, I volunteered for a digital media program called "Voices of Our Future" through World Pulse, a global organization aimed at amplifying the voices of women, especially in developing nations. This experience allowed me to form lifelong friendships with bold, creative, and changemaking women from Ghana, Nigeria, Nepal, Cambodia, and beyond. These women taught me so much about using personal power for the greater good of our communities, just by me reading their words and holding space for them to express themselves. I came to see how easily we can become a part of positive change just by extending our authentic presence with others who co-exist with us, even if half a world away.

Now as a mother to a biracial son, I am more aware than ever of the responsibility and power I have in raising a leader who will be an active and conscious participant in the community around him. It all begins with knowing that he has tremendous capabilities and that we are here to encourage and support him in sharing his best self with the world. When we attended our local marches after the George Floyd murder, I made a sign with the words "Black Lives Rising" to challenge the status quo. We are moving beyond pleading and justifying that Black lives matter;

we already know the truth that they matter. We are here to create opportunities for the Black community to *rise powerfully* and to focus on elevating them toward well-being and success. This hand-drawn sign has evolved into an apparel line, with people around the world wearing Black Lives Rising shirts, and a social enterprise dedicated to amplifying Black leadership. The Mama Bear in me again took immediate action out of love for my son, and even though I have moments of self-doubt and worry that I am not doing enough, my efforts will grow as he grows, and I will let the truth of what I know be my guide. We can be a massive force for change if we come together in solidarity of what we know: love and respect for humanity is how we grow, and each of us is responsible for contributing to that growth.

Taking On the Hard Journey

No matter how you slice it, taking on social change work means an upstream journey, whether you do the work quietly or publically, with or without a title. We are going against the grain, ruffling up what might be uncomfortable, trying new things for the first time, and bravely putting ourselves and our hearts out on display for all to see and judge. It can be daunting and energetically demanding, and there will be many disheartening moments that will test us and make us want to quit. But once we arrive at a certain point in our consciousness that will not allow us to stay in the zone of complacency, we can gather the tools and support we need to move forward with strength and courage.

After fighting off several years of harassment and racism in the workplace, my husband was discussing a new job opportunity with an associate. This colleague pointed out how difficult and challenging the role would be and gave my husband some sound advice. However, when we discussed it among ourselves later that day, my husband reminded me that nothing has ever been easy for him in his life. Those of us who have had to navigate the extra challenges created by structural oppression can use our resilience and experience to move through the never-ending obstructions that come our way. There is always a path we can find, or create, to keep moving forward.

After a decade of coaching and guiding women to share their greatness with the world, creating and leading this book to amplify the voices of women of color was a natural next step for me, but it came with its own set of obstacles and frustrations. I wanted to give up several times, even while writing these words, but the bigger vision and mission of this work is too important to let my personal discomfort take over. As a personal growth nerd who loves books, I am determined to change the face of bookshelves everywhere and to create space for women of color leaders to shine their light. Oftentimes, the things that are most worth doing are the hardest ones, and for those of us who are called, we are here to step up to the challenge.

Stepping Into The Changemaker

Turning our love for humanity into actions that will serve the world will demand the best of us. Most of us who are drawn to social change will go through metamorphic shifts within ourselves and in our personal and professional lives that we might not have been prepared for. There will be people we love who won't be ready to support us; there will be people intimidated and threatened by the changes we seek to make, and there will also be others eager for our attention, time, and energy. There will be a lot of emotions and boundaries to navigate and balance, all while we try to focus on doing work that delivers results and impact. Here are some personal practices to stay nourished and fueled along your journey.

Practice extreme self-care and consciously choose joy. When we take on work that involves witnessing and processing the injustice and heartache of this world, we must be able to not let it consume our light so we can keep going for the long haul. Personal well-being, mental health, and emotional wellness need to be top priority in our everyday lives to balance out the heavy energy that may come from doing life-changing work. We are resilient from the hardships we may endure from our experiences as women of color, but the heaviness can get too much if we aren't proactive about nourishing and refueling ourselves. Journaling, therapy, exercise, time in nature, dancing, trying new things, and being with people who make us laugh are some personal practices to prioritize in our busy schedules. Let's add fuel to our fire by being intentional and conscious about amplifying our joy!

It might feel contradictory, or there may be some sense of guilt when focusing on joy, especially when the subject of our work is so serious or when society would prefer to keep us down. The act of choosing joy and being joyful is revolutionary in itself. When I chose the words "Black Lives Rising," I was intentional about moving in the direction of a happy, successful, thriving, respected, and loved Black community. The energy of what we want to create and make happen is the energy we must adopt and embody now. And when enough people take on the energy of what we want to see for our world, we will reach the critical mass we need to actually make it happen in front of our eyes.

Build healthy boundaries and team up with community. One thing I learned very quickly when I started amplifying my voice and challenging the status quo is that people really start to show their true colors when tough issues are raised and core values are put on the table. Personal biases are revealed and certain relationships can become strained, and we may need to adjust our boundaries with certain people in order to stand in our truth and keep our peace. Our family lives in a fairly non-diverse community, and we have many non-racialized friends and colleagues. We have had to learn how to communicate or adjust our own participation when people we know are unhealthy for us. Yes, it is important to know and interact with a variety of viewpoints because everyone has their own unique perspectives. But ultimately we need to align ourselves with those who believe in our mission for the greater good and can help us strengthen our resolve and enrich our spirits.

- Do you have a strong community who believes in your cause?
- Do you have an inner circle that champions your efforts?
- Do you have personal friends with whom you can share your struggles with and celebrate your wins?

- Are you surrounded by people who will fight alongside you when you take it to the streets?

As my husband and I build our new focus and efforts toward racial equity, we are making new connections and creating new partnerships that empower us. We cannot do this work alone; social change work takes villages upon villages that span beyond borders and time, and we must nurture new alliances that will keep taking action toward an equitable and loving world.

Stay in the process and believe in your impact. I am ambitious and passionate, but I am also infamously impatient. It is an ongoing practice to remind myself that making true change is a marathon and not a sprint. I cannot expect myself to come up with one solution that will solve all of the world's problems yesterday, and I cannot give up just because I don't see instant results or massive shifts from one initiative. Every single action and effort, no matter how tiny, is essential and is contributing to tipping the scale in the right direction. Congratulate yourself for every movement made, and celebrate with your crew for every win!

Change, progress, and success start by us not sitting on the sidelines. As women of color, we may be playing in an arena with many of the rules stacked against us, but let us remember that this arena and its rules were white-man-made, and we women of color are the new players and we are here to upgrade the game.

As a mom, I am going to maximize my power and surround myself with other legacy leaders who will fight alongside me to create a better world for our precious children. Can you see a future where our children's children are grown and where there is respect, love, and synergy across all races and colors? I can ... because I am actively creating it.

Will you join us?

ACKNOWLEDGMENTS

For Kevin, we are eternally one. For Alyssa and Adam, my love for you knows no bounds. Mom and Dad, thanks for giving me a head start in life and always believing in me. To my friends and mentors, I am who I am due to your love and support. Thank you.

-Stacey Luces

To my mother and grandmother, who showed me what goodness looked like and taught me to be courageous and use my voice, and to my children and grandchildren, who taught me what love looks like. I thank you for gracing my world.

-Debra Christmas

To my parents, relatives and those who consider me a friend "The good, the bad, and all the in between; I'm thankful for it all and for you all."

With sincere gratitude,

-Angella Mignon-Smith, P.Eng

Much love, admiration and gratitude to my parents, Kay and Lloyd Pinnock, and my brother, Roger. To our extended family who experienced life in a new land alongside us, as we supported each other on the journey. And to all the families who've made brave choices to leave comfort for uncertainty, and surely have their own inspiring stories to tell. I honor your stories by sharing mine.

- Lisa Pinnock

Thank you to my mother and Lola for inspiring me to truly rise in my power with this book. May my sisters, daughters, and nieces be further inspired to rise as future women leaders of the world.

-Michelle H. El Khoury, PhD

To all my sisters around the world who remind me to be courageous and magnificent. And to my Team Smallsy loves: everything I do, I do for you.

-Lola T. Small

To all the women of color and natural born leaders who dare to boldly take on the world. You are not alone—you are lighting the way. To my father, mother, sister, niece, and "fam"—you are the wings on which I soar.

-Suzanne Duncan

I thank my Boo, my Bubbs, and my entire team for the inspiration and support to share my words. Special thanks to D. and H., who do hard things for the sole purpose of making my life easy.

-Sherry S. Maharaj

Thank you, Lola, Kylee/GBR, my co-authors, my parents, my family, and my friends.

To my greatest loves, Robert, Maya, and Edie: your inspiration and support in life and on this journey means everything. Thank you. I love you so so much.

-Dana Christina Williams

Few words can describe my thanks to those who have guided me along my journey, especially those who have walked with me in darkness and in light. My rootedness to TB; our children: Kieran, and especially Iris, my heart; and Cassie, my soulfire—you are everything to me.

Thank you.

-Gina Wong

I have so much gratitude for this experience and would like to thank my family and friends who have encouraged me to rip the band-aid off and write. It's an opportunity to share experiences and knowledge to help others. If we don't, who will?

-Dionne Bowers